To Mabel & Billy

Best Wishes

Stanley.

COMPUTER-AIDED DESIGN FOR CONSTRUCTION

COMPUTER-AIDED DESIGN FOR CONSTRUCTION

A Guide for Engineers, Architects and Draughtsmen

STANLEY PORT

BSc, PhD, CEng, FICE, FIStructE, MBCS,
Fellow of the Royal Society of Arts

GRANADA
London Toronto Sydney New York

Granada Technical Books
Granada Publishing Ltd
8 Grafton Street, London W1X 3LA

First published in Great Britain by
Granada Publishing 1984

British Library Cataloguing in Publication Data

Port, Stanley
    Computer-aided design for construction.
    1. Structural design——Data processing
    2. Civil engineering——Data processing
    I. Title
    624.1′771′02854   TA658.2

ISBN 0-246-12201-3

Printed in Great Britain at the
University Press, Cambridge

Contents

Acknowledgements

I gratefully acknowledge the assistance during the research and production of this book of a great many individuals. It is impossible to mention them all, and I humbly apologise to those omitted. Ed Hoskins of Applied Research of Cambridge, Dr John Davison and John Watts of GMW Computers, Jeff Travers of Michael Twigg Brown & Partners, and Michael Stonefry of Pell Frischmann & Partners – all read large sections of the manuscript and suggested improvements and corrections. Any errors that remain are my own. John Banyard of Severn Trent Water Authority contributed information and views for the section on mapping and public utilities. I have had many useful discussions over a period with Ian Hamilton of CICA.

Photographs, drawings and examples of output which I have included represent the work of a large number of persons. They were kindly made available to me by several professional firms and CAD suppliers, and I have acknowledged these separately where they appear.

My views on the requirements of user organisations, and on selection and management of systems have been moulded by contact with, and long discussions with many organisations. I must particularly mention in this respect the following:

Dr Wilem Frischmann and Tony Racher   (Pell Frischmann & Partners)
Derrick Metcalf and Bob Gifford   (British Broadcasting Corporation)
Peter McGee   (IDC Consultants)
John Bonnington   (John Bonnington & Partners)
Michael Twigg   (Michael Twigg, Brown & Partners)
Peter Lyon   (Austin, Smith: Lord)
Chris Blow and Roger Matthew   (Scott, Brownrigg and Turner)
Kevin Jefferson   (APT Group Partnership)
Brian Fookes and Chris Vousden   (The Thomas Saunders Partnership)
Robert Sansome   (Roger Hobbs, John Corbey & Associates)
John West   (Robert Davies John West Associates)
Malcolm Nickolls   (Nickolls, King, Davies)
Roger Broome and Michael Boyce   (J T Design Build)
Philip Serle-Barnes   (Steenson Varming Mulcahy & Partners)
Michael Miller   (North West Regional Health Authority)

Stanley Port
Monk's Lantern
Busbridge Lane
Godalming, Surrey
England.

CHAPTER 1
Introduction

Drawing offices throughout the world are striving, in competition with one another, to increase their efficiency and to improve their product. Radical solutions are necessary, and many people are turning to computer-aided design. This is the process whereby we can input, store, retrieve, manipulate, display on screens, and reproduce on paper or other medium, all the graphical information which relates to design projects.

As a technique, computer-aided design is not restricted in scope to any one industry. Increasingly there is evidence of its use in the design of aeroplanes, spacecraft, electronic circuits, car bodies, mechanical components, oil platforms, chemical plants, city plans, and individual buildings. It has been in use on a limited scale for several years. But with rapid improvements to facilities available, and with an economic situation that is rapidly tilting in its favour, no engineer, architect or draughtsman can remain aloof. There are here the elements of high reward and high risk, and two major problems present themselves to every organisation.

First of all there is the problem of choice of system. How are we to provide ourselves with suitable equipment and programs from a rapidly changing marketplace where there is almost an overabundance of choice? The right choice of system provides the organisation with a modern tool, and an opportunity for the future. The wrong choice can be expensive and wasteful of people's time, and could be a brake on further progress. But failure to make any choice is also beginning to look like an expensive option.

After selection, the second problem is how to tailor the facility to the particular organisation, and how to prepare for and manage it after it arrives. A computer-aided design system is likely to initiate some fairly fundamental changes within a firm, but the one thing it will certainly not do is to manage itself.

The key to success, as in most fields, is knowledge. This book is an introduction to the subject of computer-aided draughting and design methods. It concentrates on the practical aspects, including the choice, installation, application and management of CAD in the working design office.

CHAPTER 2
Fundamentals of CAD

TERMINOLOGY AND CAD SYSTEMS

CAD is a term which has recently entered into daily use and has gained some acceptance. It will be used frequently in this book because it does have the advantage of brevity.

CAD is an acronym. Some people use it for 'computer-aided drawing', others for 'computer-aided design'. They seem to agree on 'computer-aided', and indeed these words are a useful reminder that the computer is merely a device which exists to assist us. This puts the machine in its rightful place, for we humans ought to remain in full control. It is over the third word that confusion sometimes arises.

There are now many CAD systems available to design organisations. They vary in cost, scope, capability, and in suitability for the work of the particular office. All but the simplest systems are intended to be rather more than aids to drawing production. However none is capable of aiding all aspects of the design process. In reality, all systems fall somewhere between 'computer-aided drawing' and 'computer-aided design'. So 'CAD' will be used just as a convenient label or 'handle' for a complex technique.

Many people find that technical jargon is a barrier to their comprehension of anything connected with computers. However it is difficult to avoid its use entirely. The aim here will be to limit it as much as possible, and to explain terms when first used. We have already met the problem with 'CAD' itself, and have met the widely used but intangible word 'system'. The latter will specifically mean the combination of several items of equipment which are linked together to form the computer configuration, plus the programs or instructions which enable the equipment to function under the user's control. So a 'system' is 'hardware' plus 'software' – the equipment and the programs. A 'database' is a structured set of computer files in which information is stored.

This chapter sets out to introduce the reader to the techniques and potential of CAD. There will be comparatively little mention of computer equipment, because this topic will be covered in the following two chapters. Later, we will examine a few typical systems and discuss some applications. Then will come a discussion of the pros and cons of using CAD and there will be detailed consideration of topics such as the selection, installation and management of systems. This book should be viewed merely as an introduction to this rapidly developing subject.

THE BACKGROUND

Where there is a history of using computers particularly within an engineering design office, it has mainly been for elaborate calculations such as structural analyses, and for administrative chores. Such tasks are essentially operations on numbers, and this is work for which computers are ideally suited.

However designers tend to communicate most project information in graphical form. Drawings have always been central to the whole construction process, and are likely to continue as such in the foreseeable future.

It has taken some time to teach computers to cope with information in graphical form. But the incentives are evident. A design office might typically spend only 5 or 10% of its collective effort on calculations. However the production of drawings might well represent 40% or more of its total workload. So any improvement that can be achieved in drawing efficiency ought to have a high impact. This undoubtedly accounts for much of the huge current interest in CAD.

Although this interest seems very recent, the origins of the technique in fact date back to around 1960. This was when Ivan Sutherland was working in the USA on interactive graphics. This work gave rise to the well known 'Sketchpad' project.

Much progress was made during the 1960s and early 1970s, but it was an expensive pastime. However there was impetus from the American space programme, and from the aerospace, automotive and electronics industries. The economics of the design process in these industries was perhaps rather more accommodating than that prevailing in the construction industry.

In the 1970s, an examination of the commercially available systems might well have indicated that they were still too expensive and too lacking in practical features to be attractive for normal design office use. Nevertheless the race was certainly on among potential suppliers for a share of a big market that was undoubtedly coming.

Automatically plotted drawings produced as a by-product of an engineering applications program are no recent achievement. As an example, if we examine highway design, we find that in the late 1960s and early 1970s the geometry of most important new roads was being drawn by computer. Plans, sections and perspective views of roads could be produced automatically. However the particular programs used were limited in scope to roads only, and so were special-purpose applications programs. Moreover they worked best for long roads in rural or, better still, desert areas. They worked least well for complex road interchanges in the urban environment. Although they remain immensely valuable, such programs would not be classified as CAD systems because they lack a capability for interactive graphics. They do not permit the designer to carry on a dialogue with the computer to gradually build up, refine and modify his design information.

In building design, a similar approach of generating drawings automatically as the by-product of design programs would be less successful. It would be possible at all only for highly coordinated system buildings.

Therefore the widespread use of computer techniques has had to await the introduction of the interactive graphics systems now labelled as CAD systems. These permit the designer/draughtsman to sit at a workstation and to issue a command and other information to the computer. The computer then performs some function as instructed and displays the result on a graphics screen for the user to check. Assuming all is well, the user can proceed to another step in the process, and another, until the whole design task is completed.

Thus the user interacts with the computer. There is teamwork between him and the system. This teamwork is usually successful because the computer is adept at repetitive and mundane tasks, has a large and extremely accurate memory, can perform systematic tasks very rapidly, and does not get tired or even bored. The human is much superior at controlling the process or steering. He does this by exercising human qualities including his judgement, experience, intuition, imagination and intelligence.

The watershed for CAD in the construction industry came around 1980. It took a long time and much effort to develop systems into the robust, effective and practical tools that some have become today. The reasons are:

1 CAD systems require powerful computer processors, but the necessary power only became available in the modern minicomputer.
2 CAD requires very sophisticated programs. After many years of intensive development, programs eventually emerged with the necessary capabilities and robustness.
3 The relative costs of human labour and computer systems continue to change in favour of the latter. There is still a general shortage in most places of suitably experienced designers/draughtsmen.
4 There has been a growing awareness in the recent harsh economic climate that all organisations must make greater efforts to remain cost effective.
5 Construction projects of all kinds have been becoming steadily more complex, and must contain an ever-widening range of facilities and services. There has been tighter legislation to cope with, and new materials and practices – but often a shorter construction time is provided. When all this leads to increased size of the design team, it inevitably leads to greater difficulties in communications. On the other hand, if CAD can increase the productivity of individuals, it not only leads to smaller and more cohesive design teams, but permits a reduction in overhead costs. All this has been becoming more obvious in many design offices.

A DRAWING PROCESSOR?

People are now increasingly familiar with the operation and potential of word processors. A word processor facilitates the build-up of a document from its constituent elements. These elements are the individual characters available on the keyboard. At the same time as the document accumulates, the elements are given a structure – this being the words, sentences, paragraphs, tables and so on. The elements can be easily and continually manipulated, rearranged, deleted or restructured so as to improve the content, clarity, and usefulness of the document. There are few limitations on the nature and content of the document created. The elements are stored in magnetic form throughout. Some might be retrieved from previously filed documents, and a new document can be stored away for possible future use. The whole process is done under the control of an operator at a machine. At any time, the currently stored document can be viewed on a screen, and when required can be printed on paper.

Word processing has been discussed because there is some analogy here with a CAD system. In the CAD system, the elements can be characters, because text is a constituent of most drawings. But they might also be points, lines and arcs. The basic graphic elements can be put together in various combinations too and so given structure – the shapes, components, views, drawings or perhaps digital models of complete projects. The analogy with word processing is useful, but should not be taken too far, or it may limit our ideas on the potential of CAD.

Most CAD systems fall into one of two categories. There are first the two-dimensional (2-D) drafting systems, and secondly the modelling systems which may have some 3-D capability. The word processing analogy holds better for the first category. Both types of CAD will be described, starting with 2-D drafting systems.

A NEW DRAWING SURFACE

Suppose that instead of using an A1 or A0 drawing board we could change to a much larger surface over which it was still comfortable to work. What advantages would there be?

To identify these, consider as an example the procedure in a multidiscipline design office which was planning the ground floor layout of a large building project.

With the larger drawing surface available it would certainly become possible to work on the floor layout of the whole building at one time. We would not have to select a small scale, because we would no longer be confined by the edges of a drawing board. In the early stages, this would not be too important because there is little detail anyway. But the architect could draw some grid lines and the first tentative building outlines. Later on, he could turn his attention to various areas of the floor, working up more and more detail. This could all go down on the one drawing surface. Even though this is large, it would be easy to take increasingly close looks at any selected areas of the floor plan, and still add more and more detail such as walls, doors, partitions, windows, and staircases.

All this of course was not possible on the old drawing board. It was constantly necessary to move on to other sheets of paper. There was much copying on to the new drawing sheets of information that had been drawn previously, such as the grid, building outlines and window positions. Much of the redrawn material had to be done at different scales. This prevented much of it from being simply traced off.

Turning back to our new drawing surface, there would be no worries about which drawing sheets show the latest ideas and which are out of date. There would be only the one large sheet for the whole ground floor area. This would be the current copy and all the spatial design information that was currently available would be on it.

With the new method there would need to be some means of making alterations. Ideally what is needed is a swift method that does not depend on razor blades or erasing machines and which does not leave messy traces. It should not involve the laborious redrawing of a complete area when one small part only is to be altered. Ideally it would permit lines and text to be simply picked up and moved to different positions, or erased without trace.

Facilities such as these, and many others, are in fact available in the modern CAD system. The large drawing surface is actually the magnetic storage capacity of the computer. The floor plan is created by the architect or a draughtsman seated at a workstation. A pencil or pen is not used. Instead other tools permit the input of graphical detail and these will be described in later chapters. The floor plan is not created in a few minutes. It will still take hours to build up. But the input process can usually be significantly faster than the traditional method with paper and drawing boards, and other advantages will become clear. The CAD system permits the architect to view his floor plan on the graphics screen of the workstation. He can zoom in to any part to take a closer look.

For the moment, let us continue to think in terms of the planning of the ground floor layout using our new large drawing surface. What facilities would be valuable?

The ability to copy any graphical item from one part of the drawing, and to deposit it accurately like a 'transfer' in any required new position, would be very useful. This capability should not be limited to odd lines or characters. It would be useful for symbols, for whole blocks of text like standard notes, for components, building details, or indeed for any other graphical feature that is to be repeated. After one window or one door had been drawn, it would be desirable if identical copies could be made, and each one moved and rotated as necessary, and then deposited precisely on the floor plan where required. So it would be easy to draw one structural column in section and copy it to all other positions where it occurs throughout the floor.

If the ability to copy objects could be combined with an editing capability, then interesting new opportunities would present themselves. Windows in a building are rarely all identical. There are variations in dimensions and in other respects. Now there would be the chance to draw one window, to make a copy of it, and make alterations as required to the copy in the form of dimensions, frame sections or fixing details. This then would become a second window type, which itself could have identical copies or variations made from it.

This ability to draw one component and copy it many times obviously would be extremely useful in a highly coordinated building with much repetition. One door or window detail might be copied hundreds of times. But even in a more conventional building there might be 10 to 15 different door types, and perhaps a hundred or so actual doors. There is likely to be scope for saving time and effort, and for reducing errors in most projects. The ease with which items may be copied and updated to meet local conditions has become a central theme in the design of CAD systems, particularly of those aimed at construction work.

Since in a CAD system, all the drawing detail is actually held in the computer and can be available when required, it is possible to return to this floor plan at any time. On the graphics screen of the workstation it is possible to view the whole floor area as a single unit. Alternatively when there is too much detail, or to obtain a clearer view, it is easy to zoom in to any part of the floor. Indeed it is possible to frequently change the scale and the area of attention.

This facility stems from the fact that in many CAD systems, all the drawing detail is held in computer as actual, i.e. full size, dimensions. It is the computer's rapid calculation ability that enables the components of the view to be almost instantly transformed from full size to any desired scale on the screen. The conventional precise scales of 1:20, 1:100 and so on normally only become relevant at the end of the CAD process, when the formal plotted drawings are produced.

IMPROVING COMMUNICATIONS WITHIN THE DESIGN TEAM

With a multidiscipline team, it follows that individual designers can at different times go to a workstation and can see the details of the current project design. They could add further details or make amendments. So the structural engineer can view the architect's current intentions, and he can proceed to add details of the structure. The services engineer can see the current plans of both of his colleagues, and he can add in his air conditioning ducts or heating pipes, and so on. It does not have to happen in this or in any predetermined order. So the structural engineer might be made aware of the desired run of some ducts before he settles his structural layout. It means that each discipline can be much more aware of the current thinking of the others.

Technically it might be a very simple process for one designer to add to or indeed to change the work already done by another. Here lie opportunities for rapid progress, but inevitably there are extreme dangers as well. So to prevent misuse of these powers, it is important that some form of control is built into the software and into the management of the CAD system. Obviously agreement and much organisation is necessary, as will be discussed in chapter 12. Providing some care is exercised there is potential for improving communications within the multidiscipline design team. This is valuable because communication problems currently bedevil the design process, causing misunderstandings, excessive design costs and, more importantly still, delays and inflated costs in the construction phase of the project. However it is fair to bear in mind that some of the largest problems in the application of CAD systems arise in team management to exploit the new tool, after initial familiarisation.

CLASSIFICATION OF ELEMENTS

If more and more information of all kinds continues to be built up, a stage would soon be reached when any view would be too cluttered up with detail. There might be a structural grid, walls, partitions, doors, windows, structural beams and columns, and so on. In multidiscipline working the problem would be greatly magnified because the view might also contain concrete reinforcement, steel sections and connections, expansion joints, lights, electric wiring, switches, lifts, ducts and much else. Without some means of classification of elements and of selectively displaying elements, the whole would become a nightmare.

So most CAD systems do have a classification capability. The terminology varies from system to system, but the operator can place items in specified overlays, layers, or categories. For example all the loadbearing walls might be placed in an overlay reserved for them alone. Non-loadbearing partitions might be placed in another. Still other overlays might be created for columns, ducts, light switches and so on. This makes it possible for one user to 'switch on' or select certain overlays only. For example he could display an area of floor and show only the loadbearing walls, columns, beams and air conditioning ducts. Another user might want to display an area with doors, windows, walls, radiators and heating pipe runs. So each person can make his own selections of layers and can zoom in to that area of the floor which is of current interest.

Some CAD systems do not use a classification method quite in this way. Instead they may permit the basic graphic elements of lines, arcs and text characters to be grouped into components or objects, and these are given names. Ideally there should be some form of hierarchical naming structure, so that for example a component might be called:

STRUCTURE/COLUMN/SQUARE

Then it is possible to selectively display the required groupings of components.

Yet another technique is to name components and assign non-graphic attributes to them. Then selections of the drawing file may be made on all sorts of criteria using these attributes.

Superficially the techniques appear similar. In the hands of experienced operators, however, the freedom to select any combination of graphical material proves to be a powerful tool.

COMPUTER DATA MODEL AND PLOTTING OF DRAWINGS

All the design information relating to the full floor area is held in digital form in the computer. The user does not need to concern himself too much with the precise form in which it is stored. Instead he can think of it in the abstract as a 'computer data model'. It would normally be held in the computer's disc store and would be readily accessible for viewing at any time. The capacity of the disc store is not limitless, however, and when the design work is finished or much less active it may be necessary to clear the model out of the disc store to make room for other data models. Before doing so, however, it would be copied say to a reel of magnetic tape where it could be held in the longer term. At any future occasion, this data model could then be copied back from the tape to the disc store and again viewed or updated. Security of data and archiving drawing information will be discussed in more detail in chapter 12.

So far reference has been made only to viewing the graphical detail on the screen of a workstation. This may be ideal for those individuals who have an ability and opportunity to operate the CAD system. Many others need access to the information. No matter how ubiquitous computer terminals may become, there will remain a need for hard-copy drawings, for distributing the design information to other members of the team, to contractors, clients and others.

Each drawing needs to be specified by the system user. The extent of the complete floor area to be included in the plot must be indicated. As with screen displays, he must specify the type of elements or overlays to include, for example the grid, walls, columns, structural beams and slabs, but not the partitions, services, furniture and so on. This is illustrated in fig. 2.1 which shows diagramatically the layers of information and a defined display or plot 'window'. The scale of reproduction (e.g. 1:100) and the size of the drawing paper (e.g. A1) must be given. Then a suitable drawing frame, title block and such items as a north point are needed. These may be standard components that are retrievable from the computer store. After this, all that is required is the filling in of drawing titles and other specific information. In this manner an individual drawing is composed.

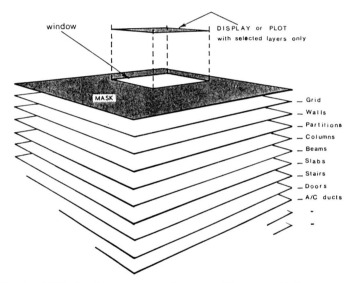

Fig 2.1 'Window' into selected area and layers of information

The ability to create some drawings at small scale, and others of restricted areas of the floor at larger scale, from the same information base is very valuable. It stems from the fact that in many systems the detail is held with full size dimensions. Then the choice of the scale can be deferred until the time of making the plot. This means in practice that many drawings with different scales and showing different combinations of information categories might be generated for the floor, and all from the one computer data model. A few systems considerably extend this facility by permitting each single plotted drawing to be composed from several details or views drawn at various scales.

Much thought is traditionally given to the formal composition of manually produced drawings. The extra freedom of CAD in this respect creates benefits and dangers. Much thought and a tight control still needs to be given to the rationalisation of the drawings for any project. Also it needs to be documented if continuity regarding drawing revisions is to be achieved.

All the information associated with each drawing can be copied to the plotting device of the system. The hard-copy version of the drawing eventually emerges on paper or other medium. The time required to generate the screen display of part of the floor might be a matter of seconds, but a hard-copy plot will take many minutes, depending on the drawing content and type of equipment used.

Drawings for internal use during the design period might be made on cheap detail paper for direct use. The final construction drawings can all be plotted on to translucent medium so that paper prints can be taken and distributed in the usual way. The computer produced drawings may well have an appearance which is almost identical to traditional drawings produced on ordinary drawing boards.

PLANS FOR ALL LEVELS

The example of the ground floor plan of a large building has served to illustrate the ability to accumulate information in many categories within one CAD data model. Some of the information is eventually destined to appear on one, two or perhaps many drawings. It needs to be input once only. This is one of the benefits of CAD systems.

This principle extends much further, however, because so far we have only considered in our example the ground floor layout of the building. Now consider the rest of the project.

The ease with which the user can copy and manipulate parts of or whole data models provides further important advantages. Having worked up some of the details of one floor, the user can make a copy of any floor areas, components, details or elements which are either identical or are substantially unchanged at other levels. For a start, the structural grid, building outlines and lift shaft may be maintained – albeit with some variations – through from basement level to the roof. Then again the same 'standard' windows, doors, precast beams and stair flights will tend to reappear at the other levels. They need not be redrawn if they are identical to previous occurrences. If they are similar yet not identical, then the previous details might be modified, or completely redrawn, depending on what seems to be most convenient at the time to the user. It is his choice.

Of course if successive floors were identical there would be no need for different sets of drawings at all. A suitable note on one set would suffice. If successive floors were almost identical, the traditional copy negative system would serve well. In most real projects, however, there is a mixture of repetition of some items and change in others. Under these conditions, the ability of a CAD system to copy, edit and locally adapt items can be invaluable.

Superficially, perhaps, one floor might seem very different from another. But even in a tiered building for example it might be possible to work first on the ground floor. When completed, a copy of this information could form the basis of the first floor plan. One or more bays could be deleted or modified as necessary. Later on this first floor plan could in its turn be copied and adapted for a higher level.

Reflected ceiling plans are easily adapted from the relevant floor plans, with such added information as is necessary to define the layout of the ceiling tiles and their fixings.

TWO-DIMENSIONAL DRAUGHTING SYSTEMS

Some CAD systems which are designed for two-dimensional draughting may operate essentially as described above. Now, however, let us look at what happens if a building elevation is required.

The elevation must be treated like any other drawing, being worked up in much the same way as the floor plans. Grid lines and outlines of the elevation might be drawn first, with windows and external doors added. Perhaps only a few window types would be needed on the one elevation. Each type needs to be drawn once only at worst. Indeed there is again scope for drawing the elevation view of one window type, and doing the copy and adapt sequence to form each variant. Each of these when created is copied into each of the required positions on the elevation. Windows created for one elevation could be copied on to other elevation views.

What applies to windows could apply equally well to cladding panels, mullions, copings and any other repeated features. Perhaps some hatching in a style of the user's choice could be applied to indicated areas of wall, to show brickwork in elevation. This is fairly easy to do with a reasonable CAD system, but is laborious by hand.

With a 2-D system, the user is therefore creating a new drawing on a new 'large drawing area'. It is an entirely separate exercise. He might use the copy and edit principle to save time if another rather similar elevation already exists. But the elevation cannot be generated automatically in any way from the floor plan. So the user needs to think out and work up the form and content of each elevation separately. He might possibly use projection lines from the plan view as an aid, in the same way as if he was drawing it by hand.

Section views through the building would be done in the same way. They cannot be generated by the computer. However when, say, the section through the first floor is completed, this might be found to be very similar to the other suspended floors. So a copy of the first floor section could be taken and moved into the required location above, and joined on. Thus the entire building section could be a stack of sections of each level, with whatever modifications made that are necessary. The roof structure might be rather different and could be drawn afresh, or maybe a few edits could be made to one of the suspended floor sections with less effort. The user can choose what is easiest. It would only be necessary to draw one-half of the length of a section view if it is symmetrical. The half which is drawn would be copied and mirrored to form the second half, and the two halves joined together. So there is often much scope for operator ingenuity.

THREE-DIMENSIONAL MODELLING OF BUILDINGS BY BOX GEOMETRY METHOD

The basis of this method is the graphical description of all the components, prior to their assembly into a complete building project.

The graphical description of each component is input and stored in the computer as a number of related views. There must be a plan view of the component. In addition to this, it is possible to add elevations and section views.

Imagine for the moment that a solid object such as a concrete beam is placed inside a rectangular glass box (refer to fig. 2.2). Plans and elevations would be the projections of the object drawn with a felt pen on the surfaces of the box. A simple cylindrical tank would become a circle in the plan view, and a rectangle in either elevation. Section views would be the projections on other imaginary glass sheets that pass through the box and component.

If all these sheets were labelled as plan, front elevation, and so on, and then dismantled and stacked together, then collectively they would become a graphical description of the component. The stack of related views would provide us with certain information on its three-dimensional form. It is not, however, a completely unambiguous description of the solid object. Nevertheless there is an important attraction. It is in practice relatively simple to draw each of the views as a 2-D drawing, and the limitations are not too significant for most building design.

When the method is incorporated into a CAD system, it relies on the user to build up a library of components. The user defines each component view as a 2-D drawing; the computer does not generate these. The user decides whether he wishes to represent the

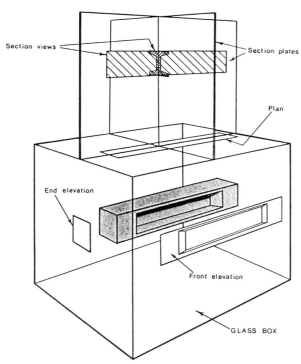

Fig 2.2 Views projected on a glass box by a component (box geometry method)

object in plan, elevation or section as an accurate representation, or alternatively as a schematic representation or as a symbol. In addition, he must designate and mark on each view an origin point for the component.

In a building, such components will include the prefabricated items brought on site and all the in situ pieces of construction.

A single data model can be assembled for the entire building. This would be done by indicating the exact location of each component's origin point on the building plan, as well as the orientation of the object. This fixes the component exactly in plan. Then the level of each component's origin must be given. This then fixes the item in 3-D space. The same component may be repeated at other locations, as many times as required.

The computer can now generate and display on the screen or plot on paper a plan for any specified level in the building. It is necessary to indicate the level together with a depth of field. These together define a zone of interest. The computer can decide which components exist within this zone. It can extract the plan view of each of these components and draw them one by one at the correct locations. The result is the required plan view of the building.

It is not as simple as this, however, for the computer must be capable of recognising when one object appears in front of, and wholly or partly obscures, other objects. It must cope with this situation by eliminating the whole, or just the relevant parts, of the plan views of all the obscured components.

Similarly an elevation of the building can be automatically generated and drawn. A line on the plan specifying the plane of the elevation together with a depth of field are required to define the zone of interest. For each component occurring within this, the computer can extract the relevant elevation view – if it exists – and can draw this at the correct location. Again, the obscuration of one object by others must be dealt with automatically. This results in the required building elevation. Also, by a similar procedure, a section through the building could be generated if the plane of the section and depth of view are given. The computer has to extract the correct section view of the component when they exist and to draw these one by one.

It is noteworthy that if an alteration is made to any component, either to its geometry or to its location within the building, then all the drawings produced subsequently will automatically reflect this change.

As components are defined for one project, a design office can accumulate these within the computer as a library. They are then available for use in future projects.

Box geometry modelling is not true 3-D solid modelling. The views of each component are limited to a few orthogonal projections. It is these that are reproduced every time. Problems can arise when the components lie at an angle to the plane of the required building elevation or section. This happens either when a component has been rotated from the main axes of the building before it was placed, or when the plane of the required drawing is not parallel with the building axes. What component view is to be displayed then? Systems try to cope by foreshortening the relevant component views. This may not always be quite correct, but it is often an acceptable solution.

The method is fairly simple and is successfully applied for the modelling of buildings and other constructions where the project axes and components are orthogonal, with relatively few exceptions. Because of the greater simplicity of description of building elements in such box models, the system is more likely to be capable of interactively reporting on 3-D spatial clashes between elements – such as air conditioning ducts running through structural columns. This can be useful to the designer as the project develops, but must be able to cope with tens of thousands of elements in the model. The box geometry method operates best at general arrangement scales of 1:20 to 1:200. It is not so useful for complex detailing. Without some additional information, perspective, isometric, and other 3-D projections cannot be generated.

Sometimes this box geometry method is called '2½-D modelling' to distinguish it from true 3-D representation. '2½-D' is a confusing term, however, because in practice it is used on different occasions for different purposes. For example, some people use '2½-D' to describe 2-D systems that have a 'layering' facility.

THREE-DIMENSIONAL MODELS

Some CAD systems enable the user to define the 3-D geometry of components. Each can then be positioned in space if the three coordinates of its origin point, and rotations from the global axes, can be determined in some way. Then a 3-D model of a whole project can be built up.

There are several ways of defining components. Solid prismatic elements such as beams and columns can be defined by drawing or otherwise describing the cross-section shape, and specifying their length. Ducts and pipes can also be represented in this manner. Components may also be defined in terms of their corners and the edges which are the connection of relevant corners. Surfaces may or may not be defined. Alternatively components can be built up from a number of basic solid elements such as prisms, cylinders and so on.

When defined by points and edges only, then each significant point of the object, i.e. the corners or nodes, will have to be defined by three coordinates. These could be typed in, or they could be indicated on two separate orthogonal views such as a plan and elevation. Then a list or indication of all the connections is needed. Thus a simple cube can be represented by a lattice of eight points and twelve lines (see fig. 2.3). Then by applying straightforward transformations, the computer could draw these twelve lines as they would appear in various projections from any viewpoint. These views are themselves 2-D

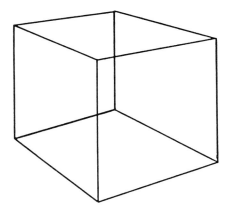

Fig 2.3 Wire frame diagram. Cube defined by corners and connecting edges

line drawings and are called 'wire frame' diagrams. Such views of complex components or of complete buildings are, however, of little practical value as they may contain far too many lines to be intelligible. Nevertheless, this is the best that can be done, unless more information is supplied to the computer.

So for an opaque object such as a cube, it is possible to define it using 'faces'. A face is a polygon with no thickness and so is like a sheet of paper. With all such faces identified and with a suitable program, the computer is then capable of carrying out the process of removing the hidden lines to produce the types of views with which we are more familiar (fig. 2.4).

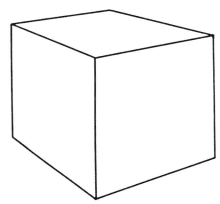

Fig 2.4 Cube with opaque surfaces defined. Hidden lines eliminated

Component description in terms of faces may be adequate for views such as external perspectives and isometrics. It is not adequate when section views are required to be calculated and displayed automatically, because a cube described by faces is hollow. So when such views will be needed, it is necessary to define the component as a true solid element, or as an assembly of solid elements.

A linear element, such as a beam or column, can be defined as already discussed by drawing the cross-section and specifying its length. A non-prismatic shape could be formed by drawing several faces that are adjacent to each other. It may be more convenient to build up a complex solid from basic solid building blocks such as prisms, discs, truncated cones, spheres and so on. With components defined as true 3-D objects and a suitable program, the computer then has enough information to display any external view or to calculate any section. Cut surfaces could be automatically cross-hatched if required.

Lines of interpenetration between two or more components can be calculated and displayed. Such techniques are generally described as 'solid modelling'.

Because each component is described more fully than in the box model, there can arise significant limitations in the size, detail and complexity of the solid model which can be manipulated.

THREE-DIMENSIONAL VISUALISATION

Some systems do not have full 3-D capability but nevertheless provide some added facilities for transforming the 2-D plans into a form of 3-D. This is to enable views in perspective, isometric or other projection to be generated. So starting off with a plan view of a building or other project, the user can add information about the third dimension. However he only has to attend to those parts of the project that need to appear in the finished 3-D views, for example, the items of the external envelope of a building.

The third dimension is added in various ways. Perhaps the simplest way is to build up construction from elementary prisms. Each prism can be given a height and is based upon a closed shape which has been drawn in 2-D on the plan view. The computer can determine the three coordinates of each of the corners, from the 2-D coordinates, and from the elevations of the ends of the prism. Curved surfaces, where they occur, can be subdivided into plane facets.

This technique allows the simple wire line views to be generated. Surfaces might need to be defined as opaque or transparent. If they are, then the hidden lines could be removed to produce the final views.

Once the 3-D data for the project has been described by this or other means, it is a simple matter to generate any number of perspectives, isometrics or other views of the different parts of the project from different viewing positions (see figs 2.5 to 2.7). Tone or colour can be added by several systems to add considerably to the quality of the views. In this way it becomes possible to create views of proposed projects which are meaningful to clients and other lay people. Views created from a succession of slightly different viewpoints can form the basis of animated displays.

2-D OR NOT 2-D?

Clearly it is much more trouble for the user to define projects in three dimensions. It is a greater departure from conventional drawing office practice. Also, much more computer processing power is required to remove hidden lines and to calculate section views. For these reasons it must not be automatically assumed that a 3-D system is more suitable than a 2-D system. It depends on the main requirements and applications of the particular design office.

As we have seen, there are various ways of describing graphical elements. One classification of these methods is:

2-D	2-D data and views only.
Box geometry	Plans and (optional) elevations and section views of components are defined. Components are assembled into a project. Plans, elevations and sections of whole assemblies or buildings can be generated (with some limitations).
Wire frame	3-D points and edges are defined. Hidden line removal is not possible.

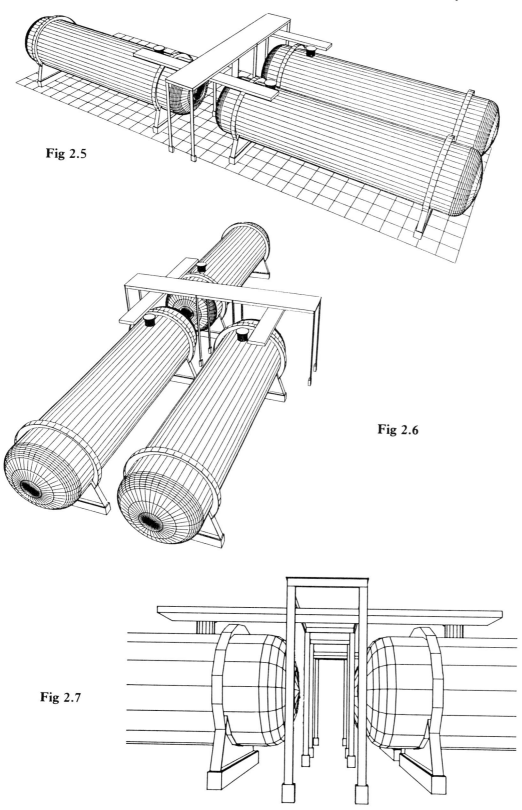

Fig 2.5

Fig 2.6

Fig 2.7

Figs 2.5 to 2.7
Perspective views generated from one data model (Applied Research of Cambridge Ltd, GDS)

| 3-D | 3-D points and surfaces are defined. 3-D views with hidden line removal are possible. |
| Solid modelling | Assembly from solid elements. Complete geometry known. Accurate sections through objects can be generated. |

For some design offices, a 2-D system may be the best choice. This can be readily applied to a wide variety of tasks including detail, and is the closest approximation to the traditional drawing board method.

Both the 2-D and box geometry methods are applied in building design.

Wire frame systems find little application because the 3-D views are of little practical use.

Three-dimensional systems, as classified above, can be of practical value when the visual aspects of the project are important. Examples of this are in landscape design, interior design, and in the design of abnormally complex projects such as process plants. There needs to be much repetition of a range of basic components. Three-dimensional views can be an aid in the presentation of our designs to clients and lay people. It is desirable whenever possible to limit the quantity of detail that is modelled, otherwise much human and computer resources will be consumed.

Full solid modelling certainly finds application in mechanical engineering. It is particularly appropriate in the design and manufacture of individual components and products. This is especially true when they are complex, but when there is not a vast number of different components to cope with simultaneously.

In this respect it is noteworthy that, in the construction industry, the tendency is towards the use of very large numbers of elements and components. It is of course a generalisation, but usually either these have comparatively simple shapes, or we are more interested in the assembly of acquired products. In the latter case, we need to indicate which item is required, and exactly where it is located. Often this is achieved by schematic representation or symbols on our drawings.

Ideally we need access to a range of such CAD facilities, so that the best method of representation can be chosen in any circumstance. This is not easy to provide in practice, and such a composite system might be far from easy to learn and operate.

This is a discussion to which we will return, for the subject is of considerable importance.

ASSOCIATED NON-GRAPHIC DATA

The emphasis so far has been on the build-up of graphical data, all of which finds its way eventually on to the drawings. Basically this graphical data describes the spatial form of the project although some of it might be text which is to be included on the drawings.

There is in addition, of course, a volume of other project information which ends up in specifications, schedules and bills of quantities and so on. Some CAD systems provide facilities for organising and manipulating large amounts of such associated data. It is already clear that such facilities can be a major benefit to users.

Associated data is information in text or numerical form which, though not required on the drawing itself, is linked with the components or graphical detail that do appear. A list of such items which might need to be associated with a sink unit shown on a floor plan is:

Component name
Manufacturer
Part number
Material

Colour
Size
Cost.

Other lists of data might well be needed for components such as window frames, manholes, cable trays, cladding panels and floor screeds. Indeed such associated data is likely to escalate considerably with the large range of components found in typical projects. So a system needs to have almost unlimited capabilities of absorbing and manipulating such information.

The essential feature is that even though this non-graphical data might be held in a separate database within the computer, there is the linkage with the graphical information to which it relates. So if the sink or cladding panel is repeated in the project, the number of repetitions is automatically recorded. When modifications are made to the design, either to the graphical or to the non-graphic database, all the drawings and schedules produced after that time will automatically reflect the modifications.

It is useful if this data can be input from a keyboard, preferably with full word processing capabilities. Ideally it should be possible for non-technical staff to do this task without them needing to have a working knowledge of the full CAD facilities. A cheap non-graphic computer terminal should suffice.

So this information is not plotted. The objective is to produce schedules, parts lists, bills of material, other tabulations, and even data for other applications programs. The usefulness depends on the ease with which the user can control, extract and manipulate the data he requires and whether he can design his own reports. What is needed is an ability to sort and tabulate the information, and to combine information from one or more drawings. It ought to be possible to sum and otherwise manipulate columns, and to input titles and headings.

These facilities are often known as a database management system. There are different types of these and their capabilities, capacity and degree of integration with the graphical information all vary enormously. They are important because they could be the nucleus of a whole organisation's information system.

The schedules are selective lists of components or materials, sorted and collated with appropriate headings and printed in predetermined formats for a variety of uses. Systems are still some way from producing conventional bills of quantities for the average project. However useful cost information can be produced to aid the designers and contractors. Certain systems are already capable of automating the taking-off and working-up tasks for projects which have a fairly limited and pre-defined set of design elements.

CHAPTER 3
The Workstation

The minimum CAD system includes the following items of equipment:

> Workstation
> Computer processor
> Disc storage device
> Plotter to produce hard-copy drawings.

Also required are the following software items:

> Operating system for the computer
> Graphics software
> Graphics database.

This chapter deals with the workstation, the equipment with which the CAD user will be most closely associated.

An early form of workstation for computers was the ubiquitous teletype terminal connected by cable or telephone line to a time sharing computer. This permitted a user to work interactively because there was a means of input, the keyboard, and of output, the printer. However it could only deal with numbers and text, and not with graphical information.

A CAD system is controlled from a terminal which we can refer to as a graphics workstation. Here the user communicates or interacts with the computer to develop his drawing. He sits here and issues commands, responds to prompts from the computer for information and monitors the current state of the drawing which he is building up.

So to permit a meaningful dialogue between the user and the computer there must be means of input and output of graphical data. To monitor his drawing, he needs a graphics screen on which the whole or any part of a line drawing can be displayed. For input, there must be one or more devices which enable instructions and data to be given, as well as some means of pointing to any position on the current version of the drawing.

In practice the elements of any workstation are likely to be:

Essential items:	*required for*:
Graphics screen	output
Means of controlling screen cursor	input
Keyboard	input

Chair	user
Surface on which to lay out reference material	user
Optional items:	
Alphanumeric screen for commands and data	output
Data tablet	input
Digitiser	input
Light pen	input
Other forms of input device e.g. mouse, voice, trackball	input
Quick hard-copy unit	output

Typical workstations are shown in figs 3.1 and 3.2.

Fig 3.1 Workstation. (Applied Research of Cambridge Ltd)

Fig 3.2 Workstation. (Intergraph Ltd)

A hard-copy unit is a device on which a copy of the screen display may be rapidly reproduced on to paper, albeit of limited size and quality. The hard-copy unit and a plotter for high quality, full size drawing output may sometimes be located at the workstation, but these two devices will be discussed in the next chapter. Here we will deal with the screens and various input devices.

GRAPHIC SCREENS

There are three main types of graphic screen:

Storage tubes
Refresh screens
Raster scan screens.

Each type has different characteristics. Storage and refresh screens are vector displays. This means that an internal electron beam is moved simultaneously in arbitrary X and Y directions so as to trace out each line of the drawing, one after the other. This beam stimulates the phosphor coating on the inside of the tube to glow.

Storage tubes

In the storage tube, the phosphor image is maintained semi-permanently and the drawing is built up by adding lines and text. However the removal of individual graphical elements from the screen can be difficult. Instead, the whole screen is normally cleared and redrawn by the computer with these elements omitted. This redrawing may require many seconds, depending on the complexity of the drawing.

Since individual items cannot be easily deleted, most CAD systems that use storage tubes deal with this by just leaving them in place, but marking them as deleted. This is done by tracing over them with dashed or fuzzy lines. Deleted blocks of text can be boxed in or crossed out on the screen to remind the user. When the build-up of many deleted items becomes too confusing, the user can clear and redraw the whole screen.

The image on storage tubes is stable and flicker free. But because of the inability of tubes to selectively delete, they are not suitable for dynamic work, for moving images and so on. They are capable, however, of displaying a very high definition image which makes them suitable for use with complex drawings. For this quality of image, they are relatively inexpensive.

Storage tubes are available in monochrome only, normally green. The image is rather dim. So they are not suitable for use in bright drawing office conditions because reflections of bright objects or windows on the screen can be a nuisance. Careful shading is necessary.

Refresh screens

In refresh screens the image is not maintained electrically. The phosphor glow fades quickly. So the aim is for the whole image to be redrawn or refreshed rapidly from a memory before the eye can detect any decay. The image should appear steady. However if the drawing is so dense that the refresh cannot be performed quickly enough, the image will appear to flicker, and this is very annoying.

The rapid fade enables graphical elements to be selectively deleted from this type of screen. They are simply not included in subsequent refreshes. It also means that refresh screens have good dynamic capability. An object can be dragged about the screen because it can be drawn at a slightly different position in each successive frame. The phosphor glow must fade rapidly or the dragged object would appear as a smudge on the screen.

The screen definition is usually not quite so good as with storage tubes. Refresh screens, unlike storage tubes, must contain memory so as to store locally all the vectors of the image in digital form. This makes them more expensive than storage tubes. Nevertheless, with the cost of memory falling rapidly, this is becoming less of a problem.

Raster scan screens

These have some similarity to the home TV set. They are available in monochrome, or in colour at increased cost.

Pixels are the elementary dots on a screen which can be addressed by a system. The image is stored in a local memory within the unit in the form of brightness or colour of each pixel. By switching on or off, or by controlling the brightness or colour of each pixel, the pattern of a drawing can be displayed. The definition is not so good as on storage tubes. Cost is related to resolution, and typically a raster screen for CAD work might have 1024×768, or 1280×1024 pixels or more. Lower definition obviously makes it more difficult to discern fine detail and indeed poor quality raster screens are difficult to use. Lines which are slightly inclined to either the X or the Y axis appear to be stepped or jagged. This jagged appearance of course relates to the screen image only, and not to the drawing data held in the computer or to the plotted drawings.

Selective erasure of parts of the image or other modifications to it is easily achieved by the computer switching on or off the relevant pixels. So raster screens have excellent dynamic capabilities. In the better raster screens the slight imperfection in definition may be more than offset by the ease with which it is possible to zoom in and out, and pan over the drawing. The image is of high intensity and so may be viewed more easily in normal lighting.

With rapidly falling prices of memory, raster screens appear to be gaining in popularity. The premium for colour is falling fast and it is unlikely to be long before colour screens are the norm.

Most graphic screens are 19 inch measured on the diagonal and this is adequate for most purposes. Smaller screens can be difficult to use especially if menus, input commands and prompts for the user all have to be accommodated as well. To conform with common drawing practice, it seems only sensible for the screen to be orientated in landscape format, that is with its longer dimension horizontal.

ALPHANUMERIC SCREENS

Many workstations have two screens. One at least must of course be the graphic screen on which the current drawing is displayed. The other could be reserved for display of commands and information input by the user, and for system prompts, error messages, and other guidance being given to the user. When no graphics are involved, this second screen could be a conventional alphanumeric video display unit (VDU) usually with 24 rows and 80 column width. Some systems do not have this second VDU, and then the information must occupy some part of the graphics screen.

THE GRAPHICS SCREEN CURSOR

The workstation user continually needs to indicate positions or to point to items on his drawing. For example he may want to indicate the beginning and end of a line he is drawing, or the position at which a block of text is to be inserted. Alternatively he might want to point at a component which he intends to move. On a drawing board he might point with his finger or the point of his pencil. But with his drawing displayed on a screen, this pointing is achieved by manipulating the screen cursor. This is usually in the form of crosshairs, or a small cross or arrowhead displayed on the screen. His manipulation of this cursor in conjunction with other actions is the main means of input, and cursor control is at the heart of most CAD systems.

The screen cursor can be controlled by a variety of devices such as thumb wheels, joystick, light pen, or using a data tablet or digitiser. Ideally a CAD system should include several of such input devices so that individual users can choose whichever is appropriate in any circumstance.

Thumb wheels are a way of generating cursor movement, by separate X and Y cursor control knobs. They are easy and effective to use after a little practice.

The joystick, as its name suggests, is a device like a little handle which can be deflected in any direction and this couples the X and Y movements together. A large deflection causes rapid movement for coarse positioning of the cursor on the screen. Then a small deflection of the joystick in the desired direction causes a very slow movement. This permits accurate positioning. Some CAD systems feature a joystick which by its deflection causes a pan across a drawing in any direction, and by twisting it one way or another causes a zoom into or out of the drawing.

LIGHT PENS

These normally operate in conjunction with a refresh graphics screen. A light pen actually detects light. In action it can detect the location on the screen of any line or intersection of lines pointed at. Usually a tracking symbol like a cursor is arranged to follow the pen as it is moved across the screen. Used in conjunction with function keys, the user can define what action the system is to take. For example he can draw a line between points indicated by the light pen, move a block of text from one position to another, or identify a component. However, holding a light pen up adjacent to the screen quickly becomes tiring.

SCREEN BASED MENUS

A partial list of the available commands may be displayed on some suitable part of the graphics screen, such as down one side. The user can activate any one of these commands merely by pointing at the word with the screen cursor or light pen. On a full size 19 inch screen, this menu does not obtrude too much on the drawing area.

KEYBOARD

A QWERTY keyboard is present in nearly all CAD workstations. Some systems and some users rely more on it than others. It works like a standard typewriter keyboard and its particular function is to input text information and numbers to the computer.

Controversy exists over its use because some engineers and architects have found difficulty in mastering its layout. Sometimes it is felt that an ABCD format would be easier. But with passage of time more people are now becoming familiar with the QWERTY format and perhaps begin to appreciate its advantages. It is particularly convenient for the input of precise information such as distances, coordinates or drawing annotation. The keyboard seems likely to remain an important part of workstations for some time to come.

An integral numeric keypad is almost essential. There may also be a row or an array of function keys. Each key may be set up as a specific key which, when depressed, causes some predefined function to be requested of the system. Sometimes function keys are simply labelled numerically, and sometimes they are permanently labelled with the function. Alternatively they may be labelled with exchangeable plastic frames, so that different key names can be used for different applications programs or circumstances.

A keyboard in combination with an alphanumeric screen could be used for input and checking of non-graphic information for a project. If available, this would avoid the tying up of an expensive graphics workstation for this time consuming task.

DIGITISERS AND TABLETS

These are devices which in appearance are rather like a drawing board but nothing is actually drawn on them. They can convert a location indicated by the position of a stylus or puck on the board surface into numeric coordinates usable by the computer system.

They are used in conjunction with the graphics screen. A stylus is like a special pointer or pen. When it touches the board surface its precise location is sensed by a matrix of wires underneath. By depressing the tip of the stylus against the board a signal is sent and the computer receives the coordinates. The equivalent position on the screen may be indicated by the screen cursor and so the manipulation of the stylus is equivalent to the thumb wheels or joystick just described. A puck is somewhat similar to a stylus in action but includes a small crosshair engraved on glass or clear plastic. The user can move this over the digitiser surface. Signalling a position and an action to be taken is done by pressing one of the function buttons on the puck.

A digitiser has other uses too. A previously produced drawing or sketch on paper can be taped to the digitiser surface. Intersections of lines, positions of symbols or features, or any other significant points may be identified or 'digitised' and sent to the computer. For example, the layout of an existing building which is to be refurbished could be described to the computer in this manner. For this type of use, a large precision digitiser is required. With careful use, points can be digitised to an accuracy of perhaps 0.1 mm on the drawing.

A digitiser can in addition be used for input of commands and other information to the computer. This is done by fixing a 'menu' to the digitiser surface. Such a menu can be a list of available commands (see fig 3.3). Alternatively it could include something like a facsimile keyboard or else can comprise an array of little square areas. Each square can have a particular function and if appropriately labelled can act in a manner similar to function keys (refer to fig 3.4). The user can issue a command or supply data merely by pointing at the relevant square with the stylus or puck. In practice the menu is usually fixed along one side or the bottom of a large digitiser, so as to leave adequate additional space for a drawing. Digitisers for this use might be A1 or even A0 size, although the latter are often considered too large for convenient use.

Small digitisers have become extremely popular and now form a part of most workstations. They are commonly about 280 mm square with lower resolution capability. In this form they are frequently referred to as 'data tablets'. Interchangeable menus on cardboard or plastic inserts can be placed on these tablets and such menus may be produced by the system supplier for specialist applications. Fig 3.5 is an example of such an insert menu for the DOGS 2-dimensional CAD system produced by Pafec Ltd. This menu is intended for general draughting. Fig 3.6 shows a menu for the BOXER solid modelling system produced also by Pafec Ltd. This includes the various solid primitives which are the building blocks for creating real solid objects. BOXER is a software system used mainly in the mechanical engineering industry.

In some CAD systems the user can design his own menus. This is an important feature as it permits a system to be tailored to the needs of a particular office.

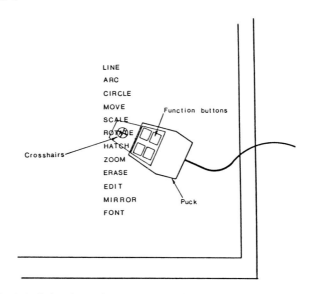

Fig 3.3 Selection of commands with the puck and digitiser

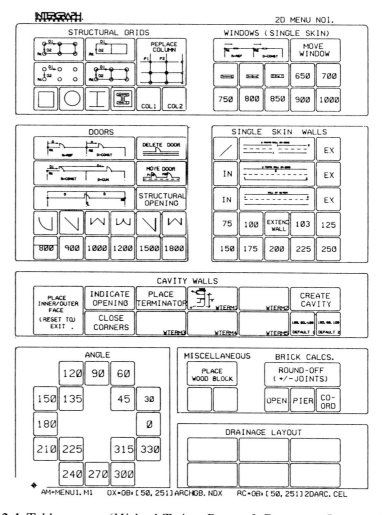

Fig 3.4 Tablet menu. (Michael Twigg, Brown & Partners – Intergraph)

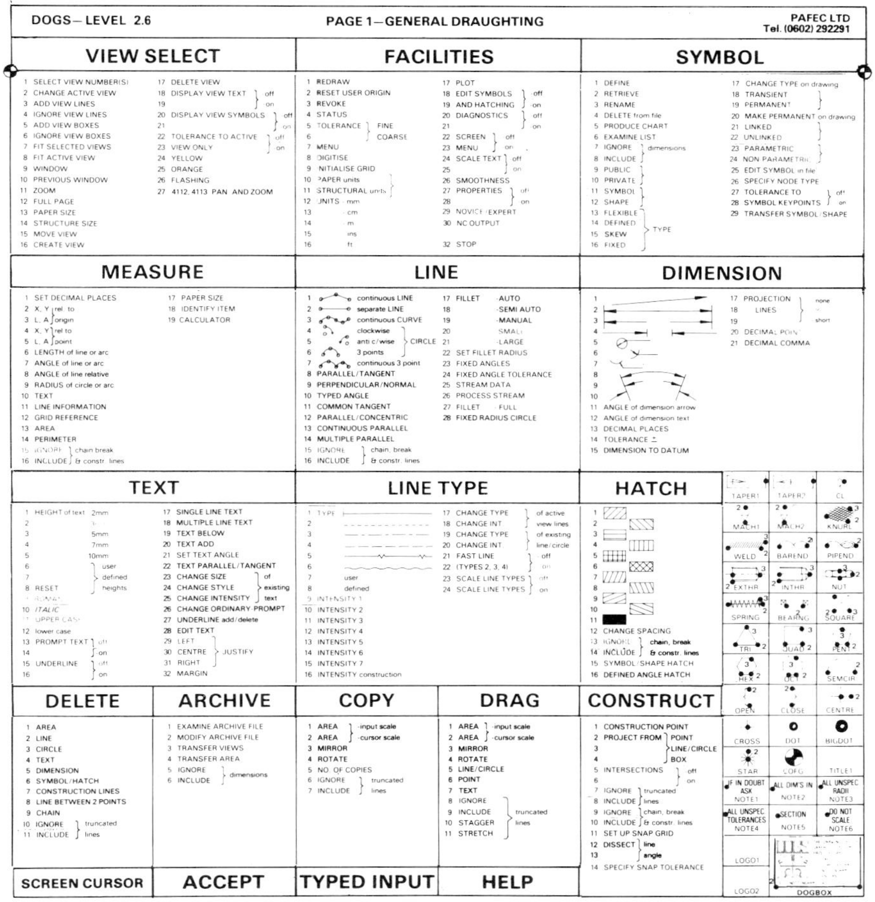

Fig 3.5 Tablet menu for general draughting. (Pafec Ltd – DOGS)

VOICE INPUT

It is now possible to communicate with a computer system in spoken words. This form of input has many potential advantages; after all, speech is a means of communication in which most users have considerable natural ability.

The technique is not yet fully developed and proven for practical use, however. Nevertheless enough incentive exists and it is developing rapidly to the point where recognition of input commands from any user is soon likely to be commonplace. Voice recognition will operate by enabling a user to speak isolated words or short phrases to a microphone connected to the computer. Initially the vocabulary is likely to be fairly limited. At set-up time, the system will have to be 'trained' to the voice pattern of each potential user.

It does seem likely to be less accurate and less flexible than other forms of input. So voice recognition is unlikely to supplant keyboards and data tablets. Its value will be in adding to the flexibility of the overall system, because it brings into use another human sense to supplement those of sight and touch. It is unlikely to be long before the system will be talking to us as well, prompting us for information, and warning of errors.

INPUT OPTIONS AND WORKSTATION LAYOUT

Several alternative means of data input have been described. Most CAD systems incorporate a number of such devices in their workstations, and adopt the most appropriate

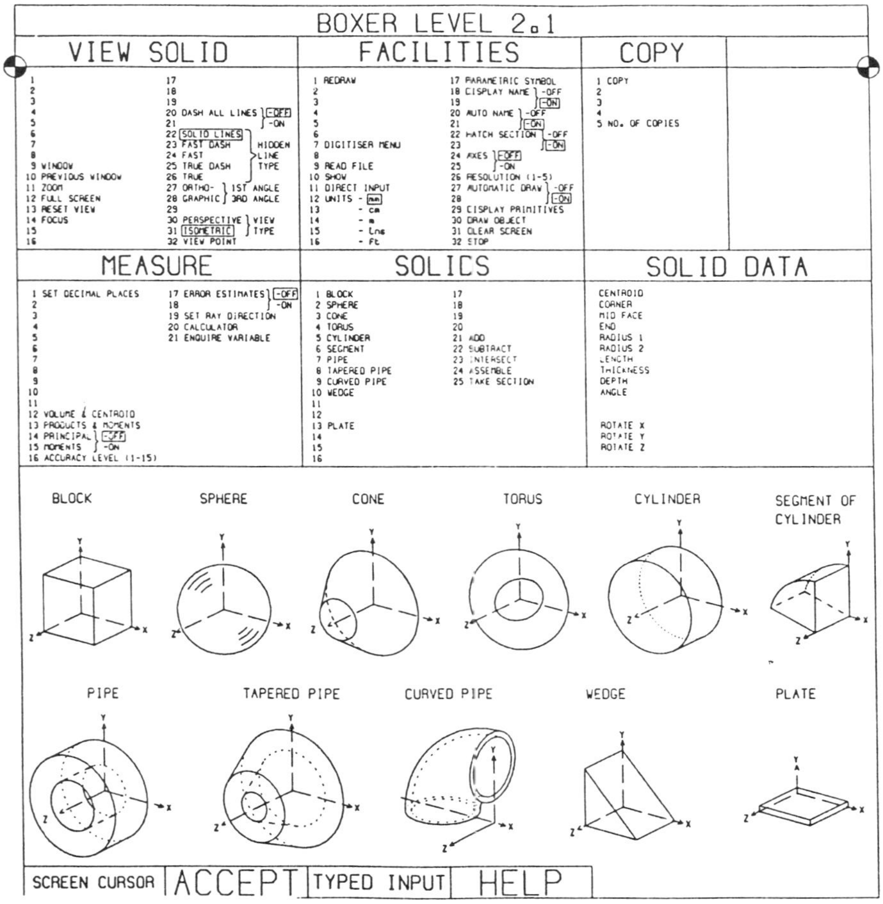

BOXER LEVEL 2.1

VIEW SOLID	FACILITIES	COPY
1	17	1 REDRAW 17 PARAMETRIC SYMBOL	1 COPY
2	18	2 18 DISPLAY NAME -OFF	2
3	19	3 19 -ON	3
4	20 DASH ALL LINES -OFF	4 20 AUTO NAME -OFF	4
5	21 -ON	5 21 -ON	5 NO. OF COPIES
6	22 SOLID LINES	6 22 HATCH SECTION -OFF	
7	23 FAST DASH HIDDEN	7 DIGITISER MENU 23 -ON	
8	24 FAST LINE	8 24 AXES -OFF	
9 WINDOW	25 TRUE DASH TYPE	9 READ FILE 25 -ON	
10 PREVIOUS WINDOW	26 TRUE	10 SHOW 26 RESOLUTION (1-5)	
11 ZOOM	27 ORTHO- 1ST ANGLE	11 DIRECT INPUT 27 AUTOMATIC DRAW -OFF	
12 FULL SCREEN	28 GRAPHIC 3RD ANGLE	12 UNITS - mm 28 -ON	
13 RESET VIEW	29	13 - cm 29 DISPLAY PRIMITIVES	
14 FOCUS	30 PERSPECTIVE VIEW	14 - m 30 DRAW OBJECT	
15	31 ISOMETRIC TYPE	15 - Line 31 CLEAR SCREEN	
16	32 VIEW POINT	16 - Ft 32 STOP	

MEASURE	SOLICS	SOLID DATA
1 SET DECIMAL PLACES 17 ERROR ESTIMATES -OFF	1 BLOCK 17	CENTROID
2 18 -ON	2 SPHERE 18	CORNER
3 19 SET RAY DIRECTION	3 CONE 19	MID FACE
4 20 CALCULATOR	4 TORUS 20	END
5 21 ENQUIRE VARIABLE	5 CYLINDER 21 ADD	RADIUS 1
6	6 SEGMENT 22 SUBTRACT	RADIUS 2
7	7 PIPE 23 INTERSECT	LENGTH
8	8 TAPERED PIPE 24 ASSEMBLE	THICKNESS
9	9 CURVED PIPE 25 TAKE SECTION	DEPTH
10	10 WEDGE	ANGLE
11	11	
12 VOLUME & CENTROID	12	
13 PRODUCTS & MOMENTS	13 PLATE	ROTATE X
14 PRINCIPAL -OFF	14	ROTATE Y
15 MOMENTS -ON	15	ROTATE Z
16 ACCURACY LEVEL (1-15)	16	

BLOCK   SPHERE   CONE   TORUS   CYLINDER   SEGMENT OF CYLINDER

PIPE   TAPERED PIPE   CURVED PIPE   WEDGE   PLATE

SCREEN CURSOR | ACCEPT | TYPED INPUT | HELP

Fig 3.6 Tablet menu for solids modelling. (Pafec Ltd – BOXER)

means for each function. Often the user can choose a method, and indeed may want to switch freely between methods according to convenience. For example he might have a menu of commands on a tablet but have just finished typing in some dimensions at the keyboard. With his hands already on the keyboard he might well prefer to carry on and type the next command rather than to pick up the tablet stylus and use this. User options in this respect can improve his performance significantly.

Long periods are spent at the workstation and so a good ergonomic arrangement is important. To ease the strain and to improve productivity, much attention needs to be paid to the selection of the components and to the layout of the equipment and work surfaces. Early CAD workstations were particularly lacking in this respect. Screen resolution, colour, image stability are all items that are important and have received much attention recently. The user must be able to easily adjust the layout and relative positions to suit his own preferences.

CHAPTER 4
Computers and Plotters

Having discussed the devices with which the CAD user can input and monitor his graphical information, we now turn our attention to the remaining items of equipment. A simple classification of these is as follows:

Central processing unit (CPU)	Runs the programs and controls the peripheral equipment.
Main memory	The immediately available storage space used by the CPU. For transitory use.
Mass storage devices	Usually in the form of magnetic discs. The longer term and large capacity storage area for programs and drawing data. Sometimes magnetic tape is also used for semi-permanent storage of information.
Plotters	For hard-copy output of drawings. Normal size drawings of high quality.
Hard-copy units	For rapid graphical output. Limited size and quality. (Optional item.)
Printers	For printing of schedules and other lists of non-graphical information.

We know that the computer hardware market is developing and changing more rapidly than probably any other. There is now an apparently bewildering range of computer equipment available. Then the individual items can be assembled and connected together in a variety of ways to form computer configurations. The objective is to tailor the equipment to match the needs and preferences of individual organisations and applications. Finally the industry has had to invent many new words, but has achieved little standardisation in their use. All these matters combine to complicate the subject for everyone involved, including even the 'experts'.

Faced with this problem, the objectives of this chapter will be limited to a brief description of individual items of hardware. We shall leave to later the consideration of how they are put together to form a configuration.

CENTRAL PROCESSOR

This is the main unit or core of the system. Acting in conjunction with the main memory, it controls all functions of the system and performs the arithmetical and logic computations. Each item in the program of instructions is read, interpreted and acted upon, and it controls and interprets the action of all the peripheral items of equipment.

Processors are almost entirely electronic, and operate extremely rapidly. Sometimes they are well able to cope simultaneously with several tasks, including the control of several input and output devices. Those peripheral devices such as printers that are at least partly mechanical in action might appear to us to operate rapidly, but in fact they are extremely slow relative to the CPU.

Processors differ very widely in their price, power and performance capability. They have been classified into three categories as indicated below. However the parameters for classification are not universally agreed and the distinctions are becoming increasingly blurred.

Mainframe
The mainframe is the traditional large and expensive computer found in large organisations, and can satisfy a variety of data processing requirements. It is often mainly used for commercial work. Sometimes a mainframe has been the only computer in a firm, so it has needed to fulfil a multipurpose role and cater for a multitude of local and remote terminals operating simultaneously. It is large, costly, complex and typically requires a department of specialist staff to look after it. It is not very commonly used for CAD work.

Minicomputer
Early minis were mainly developed for scientific and technical work. The mini is essentially a restricted general-purpose mainframe for a smaller company or department of a larger firm. It is generally cheaper, more rugged, and requires very much less management. It can however deal with several terminals operating simultaneously.

Microcomputer
The micro is the smallest and cheapest computer, and usually very basic. At the top end of the range, it can be useful for technical and business uses. Normally it can cope with one user only at a time but can be ideal for personal use or for a very small organisation. Alternatively micros can be used in larger organisations for fairly simple isolated computational tasks.

The information in a computer is stored in binary form. Single binary digits are called 'bits' (i.e. 0 or 1).

These are combined together in multiples of eight, and called 'bytes' (8 bits = 1 byte). It requires 8 bits or 1 byte to store one character of text such as A or B.

Bytes in turn are grouped together to form 'words'. The word length is the number of bits that the computer can handle simultaneously, such as 8 bits, 16 bits, 32 bits and so on.

The user of a CAD systems does not have to understand binary arithmetic or how computers work internally. Indeed the inner workings are effectively concealed from him. It is sufficient to appreciate that different computers do have different word lengths and can have different capacities of associated main memory. A longer word length normally means that the computer potentially can handle more powerful internal instructions and can process large volumes of data more rapidly.

The following parameters are sometimes applied:

Computer	Word length
Mainframe	more than 32 bits
Supermini	32 bits

Mini   16 bits
Microcomputer   8 or 16 bits

Most CAD work has been performed with 16-bit or 32-bit minicomputers. The 16-bit approach tends to be hampered by lack of power. This power is required to enable the processor to cope with a combination of heavy processing and a high degree of interaction, and still respond rapidly when several designers are working simultaneously. So there is now a strong movement towards use of the 32-bit superminis and this is being fuelled by the introduction of relatively inexpensive new models. Mainframes are used for a few of the larger installations and increasingly the more powerful microcomputers are being used for single workstation systems.

The 'operating system' of a computer is the program provided usually by the manufacturer which controls the wide variety of basic operating functions of the machine. It runs continuously during all the time that the machine is in operation. It is under the control of this that the computer drives or responds to the various items of equipment and operates all the CAD and any other applications programs simultaneously.

MAIN MEMORY

The main memory is the direct, rapid-access storage capacity available to the CPU. It is from here that the program instructions are drawn for execution, and here that immediate data and results of individual computation processes are held.

Generally, the more terminals on a system, the more memory is required. Usually the performance of the computer can be enhanced by increasing the memory capacity, and with memory costs dropping dramatically in recent times, this is a reasonable trade-off. So the modern computer has many times the memory capacity of its predecessor of only a few years ago. Main memory capacity for CAD work is nowadays generally at least 0.5 megabytes (Mb), and often 1 Mb or much more. (1 Mb is roughly equivalent to one million characters.)

MASS STORAGE – DISCS

When the computer's power supply is switched off, the contents of the main memory are lost. So everything that is wanted later, including all programs, and the drawings so carefully created by the users, must be permanently stored in some other manner. Despite the large size of modern memories, they are inadequate for holding the programs and data for the many drawings required for large projects. The problem is magnified when several designers are using the computer simultaneously. So for these reasons, every computer needs auxiliary mass storage. For CAD work this is nearly always on hard discs.

Hard discs are aluminium plates coated with magnetic medium, and are like a stack of gramophone records. They are arranged to spin at a constant rate. Data is read or written by magnetic heads as the disc surface is moving rapidly past. These heads can jump to different positions on a radius so as to read or write data on concentric tracks on the disc surface. With some designs, one or more of the disc plates may be removed, and replaced with other discs containing other information. Hard discs may have capacities of say 80 Mb or 300 Mb. A computer system may incorporate one or several such disc units.

The Winchester disc is a rather newer development and is now common particularly on smaller computer systems. It is relatively cheap and can have capacities well in excess of 100 Mb although it is normally less than this. It is a completely sealed unit and as a result is kept free from the contaminants such as dust and cigarette smoke which can prove troublesome to normal discs. Containment also means that the read/write heads can be maintained much closer to the disc surface and this improves the recording density, data transfer speed and capacity.

Floppy discs, as the name suggests, are small flexible plastic discs. They are familiar to the users of many microcomputers. They are not as reliable, and data transfer to and from them is rather slow. Capacities vary but might be about 0.5 or 1 Mb. They are however cheaper than hard disc units.

MASS STORAGE – MAGNETIC TAPE DRIVES

This equipment ranges from cassette tapes for small volumes, to the familiar nine-track industry-compatible reels of magnetic tape for large volumes. The tape lengths, recording densities and speed of operation vary. Densities are quoted in 'bits per inch' (bpi) with values such as 800, 1600 and 6250 bpi. Use of higher densities means that the tape library can be maintained on fewer reels. Speeds are frequently quoted in 'inches per second' (ips) with typical values being 45 ips, 75 ips or more. Higher tape speeds obviously reduce the time required to copy information to or from the tape, but increase the cost of the apparatus.

Streamer tape drives are now available. These give lower performance at lower cost, primarily because the expense of vacuum column drives is dispensed with.

Information can only be read from or written to tapes in a sequential manner, that is as the tape itself moves past the heads. This is in much the same manner as in the more familiar home tape recorder. Tape is therefore not suitable for retrieving information stored in a random manner because of course the tape must be 'played' all the way through until the required item is found. Despite these limitations, it remains the most convenient and cheapest form of long term storage for large quantities of data.

Tape drives are often used in CAD systems for long term storage of drawing information. The procedure is to transfer selected data to tape from the disc store, and then to transfer it back again when it is required.

As a matter of routine, tapes are also used for keeping copies of the whole disc contents as a safeguard against disc failure or other accidental loss of the information held on discs. This will be discussed again in chapter 12.

PLOTTERS

Plotters and graphic screens are two forms of graphic output device. The screens can rapidly present a rather low definition image of the whole or some part of a drawing. The user can react to and can make changes interactively. The plotter on the other hand can make a high quality hard copy of the drawing on media such as opaque paper, translucent paper or plastic film. But the plotting process is slow. So the screens are for the display of transient graphical material, the plotters for permanent records. They complement each other.

The plotter is therefore a vital part of any CAD system, being the equivalent of the alphanumeric line printer in a conventional computer installation. It is an expensive item, so there is often only one plotter in the hardware configuration and it is shared by all users. There are many types of plotter available, and the more important ones for our purposes can be classified as follows:

Pen plotters
   Continuous roll drum plotters
   Cut sheet plotters
   Flat bed plotters

Electrostatic plotters

Plotters can be driven off line from the computer, when they are supplied with data from a magnetic tape drive. However with modern computers which are more easily able to handling multiple tasks, most plotters are now connected directly and so work in on-line mode.

Pen plotters

Most CAD systems employ an electromechanical pen plotter of some kind, the drum plotter being the most common type (see fig. 4.1). In this, the paper is fed around a drum. In operation the drum rotates back and forth in either direction thereby providing one deflection axis. The transverse deflection is provided by the movement of a pen mounted on a gantry across the drum. Pens can also be moved up and down, i.e. out of or into contact with the surface of the paper. So each line and character is traced out separately, with the drum rotating, and the pen down and traversing back and forwards as necessary.

Fig 4.1 Drum pen plotter for continuous medium. (Benson Electronics Ltd).

Many plotters take rolls of continuous medium. This material has holes accurately punched along each edge which engage in sprockets. By this means the material is accurately positioned with respect to the pens. This punched material is more expensive and the use of preprinted drawing stationery is not practical. So the title block and frame has to be replotted on each drawing afresh. However these plotters have the advantages that they enable a stream of drawings to be plotted one after the other without operator intervention.

Cut sheet plotters are designed to accept individual sheets of any size, up to the maximum width. Various types exist with the sheets fixed in different ways:

The sheet is taped to a wide belt which is in the form of a loop. This moves back and forth over rollers.
The sheet is taped to the surface of a large single drum.
The sheet may be gripped at its edge by grit wheels which move it back and forth beneath the pen. A plotter of this type is illustrated in fig. 4.2.

In all these types, each sheet of material must be fitted by an operator before the drawing commences. Cut sheet plotters are ideal when an organisation wishes to use either a variety

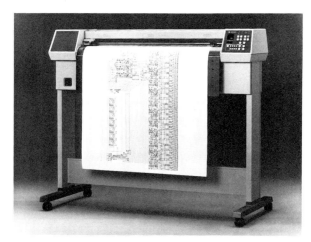

Fig 4.2 Pen plotter for cut sheets. (Hewlett Packard Ltd).

of sheet sizes, or their own standard drawing office blanks with appropriate frames and title blocks already preprinted.

Flat bed plotters are another type. The blank sheet or an existing drawing to be overplotted is fixed to a horizontal table. The pens are able to traverse on a gantry in two directions over the whole drawing surface.

Plotters may have one, two, three, four or perhaps eight pens. These may be selected or changed automatically by the software during the drawing process. Different pens might be inserted for different colours. 'Pens' can be those with liquid ink, felt tip pens, Pentels or ball point pens. Each type has its purpose, and its advantages and disadvantages. It is possible that ink jet technology will become more common.

Liquid ink pens normally produce the highest quality result and, with different pens in use, a variety of line thicknesses can be obtained. Most engineering drawings use two or three line widths only and in practice a four-pen plotter is quite adequate for most needs.

However liquid ink pens need very careful handling, cleaning and maintenance if they are not to dry up in the middle of a drawing and thus spoil the whole result. The thinner nibs are more troublesome in this respect. Dry atmospheres aggravate the problem. A pen capping mechanism which automatically caps those pens not actually in use helps to reduce it. Some CAD software systems automatically shake the pens back and forwards and plot a few characters in the drawing margin at intervals, and this too helps to alleviate the nuisance. Most types of liquid ink pens cannot be used at high speeds and accelerations. Accordingly some plotters must be operated at less than their full speed when ink is used. Other matters that have a bearing on performance are the media surface, ink viscosity, nib design and material, clearance and pressure. All these must be carefully controlled if a good result is to be achieved. Even then, failures can occur and in practice these quite often result in the disposal of an expensive pen.

Ball point pens are inexpensive and very easy to use, but require a high contact pressure. Line thicknesses cannot be varied, but ball points are useful for the numerous check plots, and for plots required for use within an organisation. In practice well over half of the plotting workload of an installation may fall into these categories.

The time required for plotting any drawing depends on plotter performance and obviously on the nature and density of the drawing itself. When comparing plotters, it is pen speeds and acceleration rates, and pen up/pen down times that are important parameters. With liquid ink, as already mentioned, the plotter may have to be operated at restricted speeds. The time required to choose alternative pens can have a marked effect on throughput. In some plotters all the pens move along the gantry together and changing pens is rapid. In others one pen has to be returned to a fixed receptacle at the side, and another pen selected and then transported to the current drawing position. Sometimes the computer processor is unable to send data fast enough to match the potential speed of the plotter.

The cost of a plotter depends on many factors such as size, speed and accuracy. Many cheap plotters are becoming available but may be capable of A4 or A3 plots only. Many of these are designed primarily for business graphics such as graphs and histograms.

Pen plotters are rather slow and noisy. They may take anything from perhaps ten minutes to an hour to plot one drawing. It is therefore important that the computer should be capable of driving the plotter simultaneously with the operation of the workstations. Also it must be possible for plots to be queued automatically within the system because a user will frequently want to send a drawing for plotting while the plotter is already producing another.

Electrostatic plotters

In recent years these have become an alternative to the pen plotter. They are many times as fast, but for acceptable quality they are more expensive. An A0 electrostatic plotter is shown in fig. 4.3.

Fig 4.3 Benson 9436 electrostatic plotter. (Scott Brownrigg and Turner: Architects)

They work by quite a different process; they print tiny dots across the width of the paper as it slowly passes through the plotter. By controlling which dots are printed it is possible for a whole series of them to form straight or curved lines, text characters or even shading tones. Typically there may be 100 dots per centimetre. Adjacent dots are deliberately arranged to overlap. This improves the line quality to the point where the finished drawing is almost equivalent to the quality of ink pen plots. The better electrostatic plots are certainly entirely acceptable for all normal project work. It requires a very close inspection of the end product to detect that the image is in fact composed of individual dots.

For electrostatic plotting, it is necessary to perform a vector-to-raster sort. This means that the drawing data, which starts off in vector form – details of individual lines and text characters – must be changed into a raster of dots. Then these must be sorted so that the plotter receives its instructions as to whether to print or leave blank each dot position over the whole area of the drawing. As there may be well over 10 million dot positions on the drawing, this sorting is a very large task to be accomplished in a short time. This sorting might be done in the host computer. However in all but the most powerful processors this might drain the computer's power away from the user terminals and result in unacceptably long response times. Accordingly the sorting is often done in a separate microprocessor specially installed for this function. Unfortunately this also adds to the cost of electrostatic plotting.

An A1 drawing can be produced in about two minutes provided the sorted data can be supplied fast enough. Electrostatic plotters are quiet and generally more reliable, and require much less operator attention. They use large rolls of media which may be translucent paper or plastic film. The media must possess a special surface treatment to make it sensitive to electric charges, and special black chemical toner liquid is needed for the plotter.

When an organisation is likely to have more than about three workstations, the extra throughput of the electrostatic plotter may well be needed, despite its extra initial cost.

HARD-COPY UNITS

Since the main plotter may be slow and could be located some distance from a workstation, it is often an advantage to have an alternative graphical hard-copy unit for producing quick plots. These might be of the whole drawing, or more likely of some part of it only, or a screen dump. The drawings would be intended for personal use or for use within a department. In these situations, lower quality and limited sheet size might well be acceptable. There may be a hard-copy unit in every workstation, or one can be shared by two or more workstations as required. Paper size may be A3 or A4 depending on the model. Some hard-copy units use light-sensitive material, whereas others are essentially small electrostatic printer/plotters and use papers treated for electrostatic use. Sometimes hard-copy units operate on the impact dot-matrix principle and then can use ordinary paper.

PRINTERS

As most of the output of a CAD system is in graphical form, there is usually no requirement for a fast line printer. However CAD systems may also create schedules of components and bills of materials. Then some form of printer device is always necessary and the quality of the end product may be important. Sometimes this printing function may be combined with that of the graphics hard-copy unit, or it is possible to install a conventional printer specially for this purpose. For small quantities of printout, a printer console used normally for controlling the computer may double for this purpose.

CHAPTER 5

CAD Systems: Operation and Facilities

INTRODUCTION

We have now discussed the nature of CAD in general terms, and have looked at the equipment used. There are many systems on the market. These vary considerably in their mode of operation and in the facilities offered.

In this chapter we shall look at some features available by reference to a few of the CAD systems that are already used within the construction industry. Different types of systems have been chosen. But lack of space precludes anything more than a fairly brief discussion of certain aspects only, rather than full descriptions of the products. So this chapter is not intended as a survey of the market, and omission of any system or a curtailed description must not be taken to indicate disapproval.

GDS – GENERAL DRAFTING SYSTEM

GDS is an advanced drafting package which has been created and is marketed by Applied Research of Cambridge Ltd. It is a software product, was launched in 1980, and can operate in multiterminal mode on either Prime or DEC VAX computers.

GDS is an example of a command driven system. There are well over 200 commands available, although about 40–50 of these are frequently used.

There are several ways in which the user can select a command:

1 He can have a range of commands set out on the data tablet of the workstation. A command is initiated simply by pointing at it with the puck, and pressing a button.
2 He can have a menu of commands displayed down one side of the graphics screen. One command is selected by 'hitting' it with the horizontal line of the screen cursor.
3 He can type in the name of the command on the keyboard.

The user simply chooses the most convenient method. The tablet or screen menus can be replaced by other predefined menus, and at any time the user can define new menus of his own for his convenience.

As an example of how commands are given, we shall look at a simple one – the LINE command. When this is issued, the computer will seek from the user two positions on the drawing, e.g. POS 1 and POS 2 on fig. 5.1, to mark the beginning and end of the line. The computer then draws the line in the line style previously set by the user. A chain of straight lines could be drawn by indicating POS 3 and subsequent positions.

Positions on the drawing are indicated by moving the screen cursor and issuing a GDS

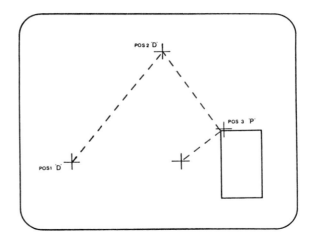

Fig 5.1 Drawing lines using hitcodes

'hitcode'. The letter D typed in at the keyboard tells GDS to mark a point precisely at the screen cursor position. Some of the other hitcodes that could be typed are:

P   Jump to the intersection of lines nearest to the cursor
L   Jump to the nearest point on the nearest line
G   Jump to the nearest grid point (assuming a grid has been defined already)
Alternatively, the user can type in coordinates.

Again he chooses the most convenient method. So the dashed lines in fig. 5.1 could be input with the LINE command, two D hitcodes and a P hit near the corner of the already defined rectangle.

That is how one element of a drawing – a line – is created. A complete drawing is built up by commanding GDS to draw elements such as lines, arcs, circles, or annotation, one after another. For example a parallel line may be drawn with the RULE command, indicating with the L hitcode an existing line, and then giving the offset distance. GDS will then automatically rule a second line parallel to and correctly separated from the first. The CIRCLE command permits circles to be drawn in any one of six ways. One way is to indicate three points with hit codes. GDS automatically draws the unique circle which passes through these. Drawings can be modified by commanding GDS to delete a line, to trim a line, copy a block of text, and so on.

However before commanding anything to be drawn it is necessary to set some drawing parameters such as units, scales and line style. Full size dimensions of the project are input to GDS and suitable scales are set for screen display and for plotted drawings. For the convenience of the user, it is possible also on the screen to zoom in or out, depending on how close he wants to look at some particular area. A variety of useful line styles, including full lines, dotted, dashed, and chain-dotted lines, in various widths and with various end marks such as arrows, are all readily available. Blocks of text for placing on the drawing can be typed in. The user has full control over the size, font, positioning, rotation and justification of such text, and he can easily edit it later. Finally, GDS permits the user to construct his own line or character styles, and to store these for future use.

There are many things that the system can do that would be very time consuming on a drawing board. Examples are the moving of previously drawn items, copying, handing (mirroring, but without mirroring the text), rescaling, rotating. To make good use of these facilities, GDS introduces the concept of grouping arbitrary collections of lines and annotation into named 'objects'. These objects may then be manipulated as individual units.

At any time, a drawing can be interrogated, for example to display the coordinates of any point, to display the measured distance between any two points, or to recall associated non-graphic data. Dimensioning is semi-automatic. The operator indicates the two points to be dimensioned. He indicates also the place where the dimension line and figuring is to be located. The system then calculates the dimension, draws the dimension and witness lines, and writes in the figures automatically.

The HATCH command is available to automatically fill in any indicated closed area with a style of lines or symbols defined by the user.

Editing is facilitated with a whole batch of commands. The following are some of the operations which are possible on lines, objects or blocks of text:

MOVE	line	object	text
MIRROR	—	object	text
DELETE	line	object	text
REPEAT	line	object	text
ROTATE	line	object	text
SCALE	—	object	text
Change LINE STYLE	line	object	—
Change CHARACTER STYLE	—	object	text
Change OWNING OBJECT	line	object	text
Change JUSTIFICATION	—	—	text
Change END MARK of line	line	—	—

'Windowing' is a facility which is available in many CAD systems. This is to set up a view of part of a drawing, either for viewing on the screen or for plotting. The extent or area of the data model which is required, and the centre of interest are indicated. In GDS the user can select the contents of the view by identifying the objects or object classes which are eligible for inclusion. The parameters which define the window can be stored if required for subsequent use. This is analogous to a layering facility.

A feature called Multiplot permits the user to assemble several views or windows from any existing drawings. These views are displayed on the screen, where they can be repositioned relative to one another. They may also be rescaled or rotated individually. So new drawings can be rapidly assembled by calling on information already developed and stored. When a new drawing has been assembled interactively, it may be plotted directly, or alternatively can be stored as a new drawing.

There is a facility for storing and retrieving non-graphic information, called GDS Attribute Data. Descriptions can be linked with anything drawn as an object in a GDS drawing. So it is possible to attach a cost, material or manufacturer to an object. As the objects are repeated or reused, their descriptors are repeated. This enables objects with their properties to be automatically tabulated as schedules, parts lists, costings and so on. Descriptors can be attached to specific versions or to specific occurrences of objects. Apart from this, it is possible to attach descriptors to the drawings themselves. These might be the drawing number, amendment, author and so on. Descriptors can be text, codes or decimal numbers and so on. Reports can be generated and printed by the user, and in these the information can be sorted, summed and tabulated according to his requirements.

GDS Macro Basic permits a user to develop his own programs to perform special tasks such as to extend complex editing and to perform calculations on graphical data contained in drawings or held in the arbitrary data facility. Again, families of components which differ only in their dimensional characteristics may be generated automatically, as could sets of drawings which have many features in common. Macro Basic consists of the standard BASIC programming language which can be interspersed with calls to GDS commands and functions.

As GDS is basically a 2-D system, it does not differ conceptually too much from traditional methods of drawing on a board. It is very comprehensive and contains many features not mentioned above.

There is an add-on package for 3-D viewing (refer to figs 2.5 to 2.7). First the user can make transformations from two-dimensional drawing to a 3-D model. This is useful in a system which is designed for use primarily for production of 2-D drawings, but also when occasional perspective or other 3-D views are desirable. Any 2-D object drawn with GDS can be identified by pointing to it with the screen cursor. Then specific data about the third dimension is added using the 3-D viewing options. Thus, a PRISM command extends any 2-D profiled as a prism to the required height. REVOLVE creates a solid of revolution from any GDS object used as a profile. It is possible to create various degrees of solidity of generated shapes, either as an open wire frame, with opaque sides and open ends, or as true solids. The division of arcs into cylindrical surfaces and facets is also under control. When the 3-D version of the data model has been built, the view from any eye position can be generated automatically in a variety of projections, with or without suppression of hidden lines. Any view obtained in this way can be plotted, or using Multiplot it can be included within 2-D drawings.

A command driven system tends to be less easy to learn than say a menu driven system. This is because there are more options for the next step, and so there can be less prompting to the user. Commands give flexibility. There can be several different ways of accomplishing any given task, and some will be more efficient than others. So the user has to think more. But this means that there is more scope for inventiveness on his part. Command driven systems therefore tend to be more flexible in operation, faster to apply, and more productive when used by an experienced operator. They are not so suitable for the occasional user.

GDS is orientated towards the construction industry. Its capabilities extend from maps, utilities layouts, siteworks, survey plots and general arrangement drawings to construction and mechanical details. It is widely used by architects and civil, structural and building services engineers.

RUCAPS – BUILDING MODELLING SYSTEM

RUCAPS is a component based modelling system produced by GMW Computers Ltd. First introduced in 1976, it has been created mainly by architects and engineers for building design. The aim was to improve the efficiency of production of drawings and schedules. It adopts the 'box geometry' principle which has been outlined in chapter 2. However, as we shall see, it provides for the full range of representation from 2-D, through box geometry, to solid modelling. All can operate from the same data model.

RUCAPS operates as a multiterminal system on Prime computer or a single-user system is available based on a DEC processor. Each workstation incorporates a large digitiser board and either a high-resolution refresh or raster screen.

Each component of a building is described by drawing a plan view, and optionally up to two elevations and up to two sections. Fig. 2.2 illustrated the principle. Text can be added to any of these views, and if required a cost can be attached so that some scheduling can be done. Each component is ascribed to a category. This is for the generic group classification to permit expression or suppression of the component in particular drawings. Up to 999 categories are available, and a design office can set up its own system for these, based perhaps on the CI/Sfb indexing system. This information is held in the component catalogue for the project. Component data can be retrieved for a project from a library of components built up previously by the office.

The building model is then assembled from the components. In RUCAPS this is usually helped by placing a drawing of the building plan on the digitiser. When each component is called up, its plan view appears in the corner of the screen. With the aid of the digitiser pen and commands, it can be dragged across the screen, handed or rotated if necessary, and placed into its correct position with an accuracy of 1 mm or better at full scale. If required it can be locked into position on a predefined planning grid. The level in the building of the component's origin point is also specified, and so its location in 3-D space is defined.

As this can be done interactively, with the current situation always displayed on the screen, adjustments and corrections can be made when necessary. A major benefit to the designer is his ability to rapidly switch over from a plan view on the screen to an elevation or section view of the building. To do this, the 'window' facility is available to dictate the extent of the required view and the categories of components to be included. This ability to flip between plan and elevation greatly assists him to coordinate his design. When a component is placed or moved, its relationship with others can be viewed immediately.

RUCAPS permits the subassembly of several related components into a 'supercomponent'. For example, in a hotel project, all the components that form a hotel bedroom unit could be grouped into a supercomponent. Then as single units these could be moved or repeated within a multistorey building. It is also possible to select any rectilinear volume of the assembled building and to copy the whole, or certain categories of components within it, to another position. In doing so, the volume can be rotated in plan or handed.

RUCAPS has other types of elements such 'stretchable' and 'multidimensionable' components. Stretchables are for building elements such as in situ beams or partitions where the principal dimension in one plane is variable. This is set during assembly of the component into the building model. It is only necessary to indicate the two points between which it is stretched. Up to three separate lengths in a multidimensionable component are stretchable and specified at the assembly time. These variable lengths can be in any plane, and this feature is useful for items such as ducts, pipework, and windows. Text can also be added into the building model directly.

The drawing catalogue of RUCAPS contains definitions of each of the required drawings. Each drawing is given a name and is specified in terms of building name, level, area, scale, categories to be included or excluded, and so on. This specification is stored so that a hard-copy drawing can be plotted later when required. A sheet catalogue extends this idea further by holding a definition of the physical drawing sheets. The user can define a sheet as being an assembly of drawings – plans, elevations and sections – on a chosen size of paper. Plotting requests make reference to these drawing and sheet catalogues and enable a whole set of drawings to be generated for output on the plotter. Priority can be indicated so as to establish the order in which the sheets are to be plotted.

As the data is all extracted from the data model at the time of plotting, it follows that the information on all drawings produced at a given time, on plans, elevations and sections, is entirely consistent. It reflects the current state of the building design. This must be an advantage. If a component is added, moved or deleted in a single command, this shows up on all drawings subsequently produced. Fig. 5.2 includes house plans and section views which have been produced with the Rucaps system.

Components are dated when they are entered or altered in the building model. This permits drawings to be produced which show components which are either added, moved or deleted between any two dates. This raises the possibility of doing drawings for checking purposes, and of producing record drawings showing modifications made during the construction stage.

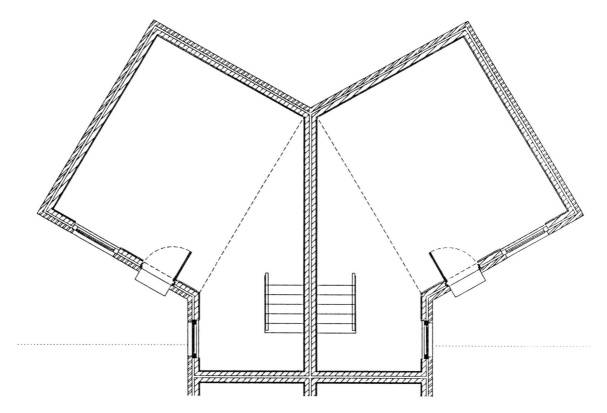

GROUND FLOOR PLAN OF UNITS A & B

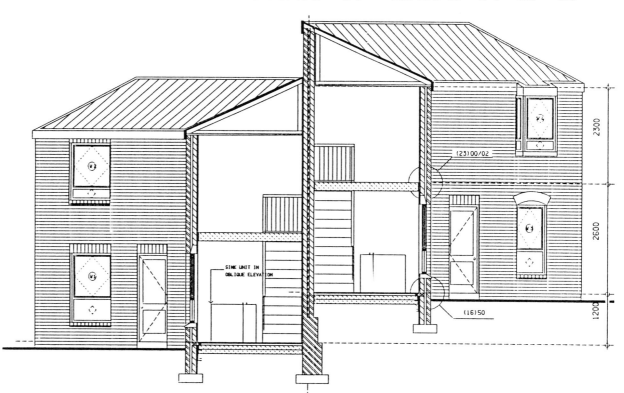

SINK UNIT IN
OBLIQUE ELEVATION

(23)00/02

(16)50

2300

2600

1200

SECTION THROUGH UNITS A & B

Fig 5.2 Plans and section views (GMW Computers Ltd, RUCAPS)

With the omission of elevation and sections from the component catalogue, RUCAPS would effectively operate as a 2-D system. For each component, the user can decide whether to include the other views. If he omits a section view of a suspended ceiling panel, then these panels will simply not appear on a section view of the building. So he adds component views if he feels that they are worth having. It is a box geometry system, and this involves some limitations as discussed in chapter 2, especially when sections or elevations are not orthogonal. However RUCAPS can deal with non-orthogonal cut lines of sections and copes by foreshortening the views in the appropriate manner. Normally any resulting misrepresentation is not serious. This point is well illustrated in Fig. 5.2. Dogleg cut lines can be defined where they are made up from a series of straight section lines.

In elevations or sections, the system has to eliminate detail that is obscured by components in front. In RUCAPS such obscuration conforms exactly to the outline of the component. However it also copes with holes within the outline through which detail behind may be observed. Fig. 5.3 is an example of an end product of this process.

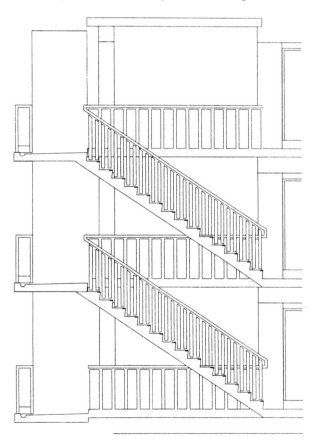

Fig 5.3 Obscuration of components by others (GMW Computers Ltd, RUCAPS)

An additional 3-D package is available for RUCAPS. With this installed, additional data to complete the full 3-D description of any component can be entered into the same component catalogue. The data for a component is input numerically by use of solid graphic primitives such as boxes, discs, prisms, tubes, bends, tees and so on. These are dimensioned and assembled to form the complete item. Surfaces can be defined as opaque or transparent. When such components have been defined, they may of course be retrieved and reused or adapted for the same or other projects.

The object of defining components in full 3-D is to enable projections of the project to be generated for display or plotting. Obscured lines are suppressed or shown dotted. Lines of interpenetration of faces, and sectioning of the entire project on any plane, are likewise possible. As with component elevation and section views, the user has the option of entering 3-D data for individual components. If he chooses not to do this, the particular components will simply not appear on 3-D views. This is an important option, because it means that he can go to the trouble of describing only those important components that he needs to be able to see on the 3-D views. Examples would be the external windows and doors, and the cladding panels when external views only are required.

With a suitable colour screen, the surfaces of the view can be shown in colour. If a sun position or light source relative to the model is defined, the gradation of tints and hues can be calculated and displayed, giving a considerable degree of reality to any scene. Fig. 5.4 is a monochrome reproduction of a fully coloured interior view created with the RUCAPS system. The colour is not just an infill between lines. It is an attribute given to each surface. This is an important distinction because it means that the displayed colour of each surface can be modified automatically to take account of the light position and, if the program has the capability, to calculate and display shadows.

Fig 5.4 Treatment of surfaces in 3-D view (GMW Computers Ltd, RUCAPS)

Schedules of components placed in the building model may be obtained. These are lists of components, under category headings, and the number of occurrences. If a cost had been attached to each component, then these would be multiplied up and totalled to give cost totals. Stretchable and dimensionable components are also listed, with the total lengths of all placements calculated. They are costed on a unit length basis.

INTERGRAPH

There are two main software packages in the Intergraph system:

1 IGDS (interactive graphics design software) provides a set of general-purpose design and draughting tools for the construction, editing and manipulation of any type of drawing element. It is totally independent of particular applications.
2 DMRS (data management and retrieval system) is the means of managing non-graphic information which can be associated with the drawing elements. It is a network database management system.

Any part of a design or drawing can be stored in the IGDS system as a discrete component or 'cell' and rapidly accessed for use in subsequent projects. At the beginning of a project, the user must set up his database in either 2-D or full 3-D format.

Intergraph is a multiterminal system and the software runs on the DEC PDP-11 and VAX range of computers. These are unmodified but the hardware system is enhanced by Intergraph who add on a graphics processor and a file processor to improve performance. Despite these additions, Intergraph have adopted the standard DEC operating systems so it is possible for the machine to be used for other purposes in addition to CAD.

There are a range of workstations available. These can have two graphics screens. This means that two drawings, or two views of the same drawing, can be displayed simultaneously. For example, one screen can show a detail while the other shows a small scale general arrangement. This is a useful feature. It can be extended, because either screen can be divided into four parts if required. So three orthographic views and a perspective view of some item could be displayed simultaneously on one screen.

Intergraph's policy is to include some intelligence in each workstation so as to take load from the central processor. The raster screens can be monochrome or colour, and can be supplemented by a data tablet, or a normal or high precision digitiser.

Geometric coordinates are held at high precision of 1 part in 4 billion, equivalent to 1 mm in 4000 km. This makes the system suitable for very large sites and for mapping applications.

The system may be operated at a number of levels:

1 The 'primitive' IGDS commands can be issued interactively by the user. In this, he can be assisted with the display of screen menus, called tutorial displays.
2 Function keys, or the keys on the puck of the data tablet, may be programmed for specific commands, user produced commands or combinations of commands.
3 Menus can be created by users for the data tablet. These may contain commands or calls for user defined cells or components from a library. An example of such a menu is in fig. 3.4.
4 Commands can be composed into programs with the aid of a command language. So a user can create facilities to automatically draw a brick cavity wall between two defined points, or to insert a door of specified size and type into an existing cavity wall. Fig. 5.5 is a drawing of precast brick faced concrete arch units. It is one of a set of twenty-five such drawings produced using a program written in the user's command language of the Intergraph system. The designer is prompted for opening width, height, arch height and so on, and the program calculates and adjusts the number and dimensions of the special voussoir bricks. Such command language programs can be integrated with Fortran language routines to form applications packages.

A specialist architectural and engineering drawing package and a space planning package have been created. These too are based on component libraries, high level

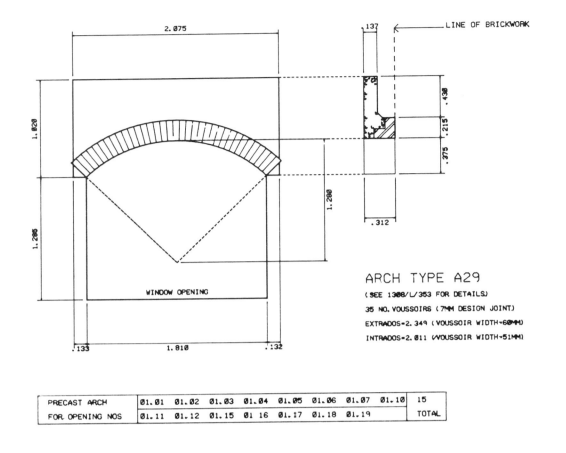

Fig 5.5 Details of brick faced arches. Drawing created using command language program
(Michael Twigg, Brown & Partners, Intergraph)

commands created with the command language, and specialised menus for the data tablet.

ACROPOLIS

Starting in 1981, Acropolis was developed on the Hewlett-Packard 3000 series computer from the original CARBS system. It is a 3-D modelling system marketed in the UK by BDP Computing Services Ltd, and elsewhere by BDP in partnership with CARBS Ltd. Objects can be created using lines, faces, solids and pipes. Solids can be defined either by a 2-D closed polygon which is extruded into a prism, or by combining faces that are adjacent to one another. When a library of 3-D objects has been created, they can be retrieved and assembled into the building. Apart from plans, sections and elevations, viewing can be in perspective, or isometric projection from any viewpoint.

Drawings are created by combining several views at any scale. These can be correctly positioned on the screen, annotation added and then sent to the plotter (refer to figs 6.8 to 6.10.

Any sequence of commands can be collected for repetitive operations and stored in command files for use in the future.

CALCOMP SYSTEM 25

Calcomp is part of the American Calcomp-Saunders organisation which is best known for the manufacture and supply of computer graphics hardware such as plotters and graphics screens. In addition, Calcomp has developed and markets a complete CAD system called SYSTEM 25.

Each workstation has a raster screen, alphanumeric VDU, menu tablet, keyboard and joystick. But each workstation also contains two Motorola 68 000 microprocessors, memory and 20 Mb Winchester disc. With these, it is capable of acting as a full CAD system entirely on its own. Alternatively, it can be linked with other similar workstations by networking arrangements so that data can be shared between users.

System 25 is a menu-driven system. Groups of commands are displayed on the VDU screen. When one command is selected using the tablet or keyboard then another special menu of available parameters is displayed so that the user can select the option he next requires. The graphics screen has good dynamic properties of panning over, or zooming in and out of, the drawing. These operations are controlled by the joystick.

There are specialist packages for architects and engineers:

Architectural Design Package (ADP)
This is a set of design drawing tools for creating and revising drawings.

Architectural Visualisation Package (AVP)
This is used to create perspective and isometric drawings of buildings or design concepts.

Architectural Production Package (APP)
This enables lists of components and materials to be taken off using the CI/Sfb system.

Architectural Costing Package (ACP)
This extends the above to the provision of detailed production cost information.

Facilities Planning and Management Package
This assists the architect to plan the layout of buildings horizontally and vertically using optimising algorithms.

Mechanical Design Package (MDP)
This is an HVAC package which is for the interactive design of complex ductwork, automatic sizing and load balancing.

CADRAW

This is a 2-D general-purpose draughting system produced by Ove Arup Partnership and which operates on the ICL PERQ workstation. The workstation includes a graphics screen, data tablet and keyboard, but in addition it contains a processor unit, memory, fixed Winchester disc plus a floppy disc unit (see fig. 7.1). When a plotter is linked, all the components of a CAD system are present. So the workstation can stand alone and function as a self-contained unit, i.e. it is an 'intelligent' workstation.

All drawing work is automatically stored within the workstation and drawings can be archived and permanently stored on the floppy discs. When there are several such workstations in an organisation, data can be transferred using the floppy discs. Alternatively it will be possible to link the workstations to a local area network. This means that one workstation can communicate with others and share data or specialised resources with them at a speed comparable with disc data transfer rates.

Apart from the facilities commonly found in 2-D systems, Cadraw has a highly developed feature for variable parameter components. These are defined with certain dimensions left as variables, and other dimensions defined in terms of these. When the component is used later, the user specifies the variable dimensions and the others are calculated by the system. These elastic shapes are useful for defining families of similar components. The variable parameters can in addition be combined with mathematical functions, and this allows the user to 'program' his own drawing components. This would be useful in practice for items like precast concrete units or standard steel sections.

CHAPTER 6
Some Applications

INTRODUCTION

CAD methods are already used in a wide variety of design work in the construction industry. It is impossible to cover all areas and interests. Instead some observations and principles will be set out under the headings:

Building design
Civil engineering, ground modelling and highway design
Site surveys, mapping and utilities
Reinforced concrete detailing
Steel detailing
Plant design
Visual impact of projects on environment.

Before this however, we will start with a very brief mention of some of the main applications in other industries. This will serve to put the construction industry uses into context.

OTHER INDUSTRIES

Electronics

CAD is very widely used for the design and layout of printed circuit boards (PCBs). This is usually a 2-D activity where standard components have to be placed at optimum positions so that the many connections can be accommodated, and these must conform to rules laid down. Colour screens are already widely used. These are required so that the connections can be readily recognised as being on the front or the back of a board. The connections are densely packed and indeed are sometimes in several layers. Output is usually to accurate photo-plotters.

The design of integrated circuits on silicon chips nearly always has to be done with the aid of CAD methods. In some ways it is similar to PCB design, but on a much smaller scale, and the patterns are much denser. Again in principle it is a matter of combining standard components and making the connections. Systems are sometimes capable of verifying that all the connections have been made, and of simulating the operation of the circuits. When the design is complete, output can be to magnetic tape for transfer to the machines that will manufacture the circuits.

Electrical

Entire circuits of say, distribution networks, can be drawn on screens. The computer can calculate the response of the circuits to various inputs. The effects of changes are easily observed and so some degree of optimisation is possible. Analysis is an important part of the work. CAD use for electrical machines has some similarity with mechanical engineering applications.

Mechanical engineering

CAD has been widely used in the aerospace and car manufacturing industries, and is gaining ground in many other areas of manufacturing industry. Surface modelling is important in the design of such diverse items as car bodies, turbine blades and shoes. The assembly of many components into highly complex structures using full 3-D modelling, and their subsequent analysis by finite element techniques, is of course particularly relevant in aeronautical work. It is useful to be able to investigate the design of complex mechanical components using solid modelling methods. Computer-aided manufacture (CAM) is the extension of these processes directly into manufacturing by transfer of geometric and other data in a form that production machines can understand and automatically act upon.

Cartography

Maps held in digital form have many advantages. They can be created more easily from new land surveying instruments or from aerial photographs using stereodigitising workstations. Maps of land and sea need to be updated frequently to keep pace with the changing face of the world, and with our expanding knowledge of it. We have already discussed the ease with which CAD data models can be manipulated and edited, and of course the same applies to digital maps. Non-graphic databases give an ability to link large volumes of information with the graphical features which appear on plotted maps. Indeed in most mapping applications this is a benefit, and the methods of manipulating this information need to be highly refined. The ability to use layering facilities is of major significance. This permits different classifications of information to be superimposed in various combinations for display or plotting.

Most mapping is essentially a 2-D activity. However there is increasing use of full 3-D facilities in for example defence applications and in exploration for oil, gas and minerals. In oil exploration there are largescale but specialist uses where 3-D models of ground structures have to be created using large amounts of seismic data in combination with information from well drilling logs.

BUILDING DESIGN

In chapter 2 the use of CAD was illustrated by reference to building design, and particularly to general arrangement (GA) drawings. This was appropriate since this is probably the most common application of CAD in construction work. Several disciplines are involved and, since they interact with one another in a complex manner, it is hardly surprising that design alterations are so common.

Much of the same graphical information of the general arrangement has to be presented over and over again, albeit at different scales and in different contexts. Thus for example we might see the structural grid, building outlines, columns, staircases, and partitions reappearing on drawings for:

Architectural general arrangements
Fittings and finishes drawings

Reflected ceiling plans
Room numbering plans
Furniture layout plans
Structural general arrangement drawings
Structural outlines and details
Reinforced concrete detail drawings
Plumbing services drawings
Heating and cooling services
Ventilation and air conditioning services
Controls installation drawings
Sprinkler system drawings.

Figs 6.1 to 6.4 are examples of architectural GA drawings for a large building to illustrate this point, and to show what is possible with a CAD system. Fig. 6.5 illustrates part of a door schedule for the same area of the floor. Figs 6.6 and 6.7 show elevation and section views created as 2-D drawings of a quite different type of building.

Use has traditionally been made of tracing or the copy negative method for copying some of the detail. But this works once only, and does not cope with differing scales.

Where architects, and structural and building services engineers all work under the same roof or have access to the same computer configuration, the situation is indeed ideal. However the industry is very fragmented and this does not happen very often.

When the various designers are working in separate firms but each uses the same type of CAD system, the situation is still satisfactory. This is because at agreed times, they would be able to transfer copies of the current data model on exchangeable discs or magnetic tapes. If the project is large or the cooperation of a fairly long term nature, then telecommunication links for data transfers could be installed between their offices.

Unhappily, the situation is rarely so convenient. Where any two contributors to the design are in fact using CAD at all, the probability is that they will be using different types of systems. Then the transfer of information on anything other than the hard-copy drawings may be impossible. This problem is being encountered more and more frequently, and is a result of both the traditional structure of the industry and the present incompatibility of most of the CAD systems. Little perhaps can be done about the industry, but there is hope that system designers will make their systems more compatible by adoption of such standards as IGES (International Graphics Exchange Standards). Eventually perhaps this rapidly emerging problem will be eradicated with such standards.

A building is of course an assembly of some in situ construction and many premanufactured standard components. When we consider the vast number of components included in a typical building, the essential aim of design documentation is to identify in each case which component is required, and its precise intended location. We are rarely designing the components themselves. Normally their exact 3-D form does not matter too much and does not have to be shown in much detail. So it is conventional to represent little more than the shape of the component outline in plan provided that this makes the item reasonably recognisable. For example, a wash hand basin only requires its outline shape, and a suggestion of the bowl, in plan view. If the outline is accurate in size, then the component can be placed on a building plan with reasonable confidence that it will not clash with other elements in the vicinity.

When a CAD system is in use, the components in a building are rarely so tightly packed that a 2-D, or perhaps a box geometry, representation is going to lead to many problems of clashing components. Full 3-D representation might be more necessary in the design of a car where component shapes are more critical. But for buildings, 3-D representation for

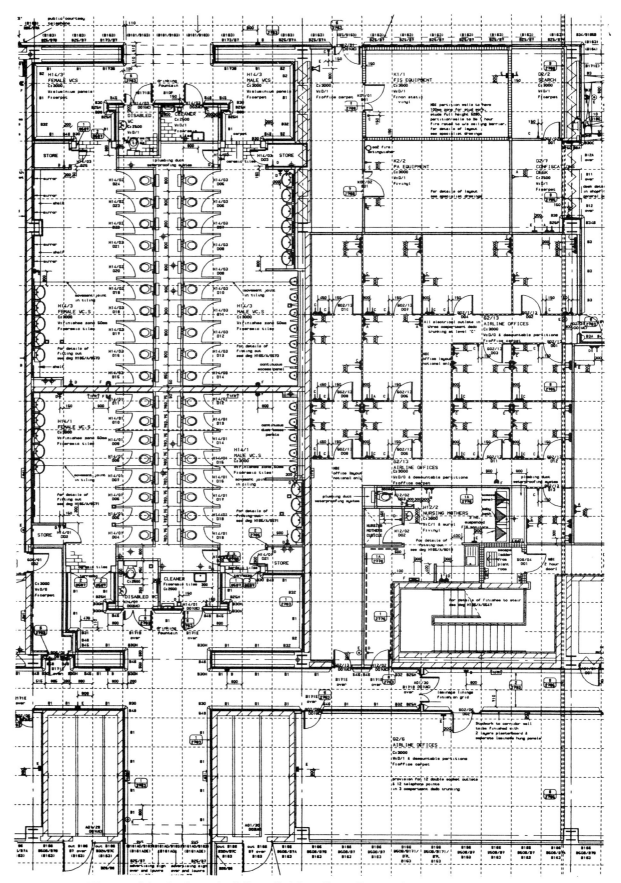

Fig 6.1 GA of a large building: finishes (Scott Brownrigg and Turner, GDS)

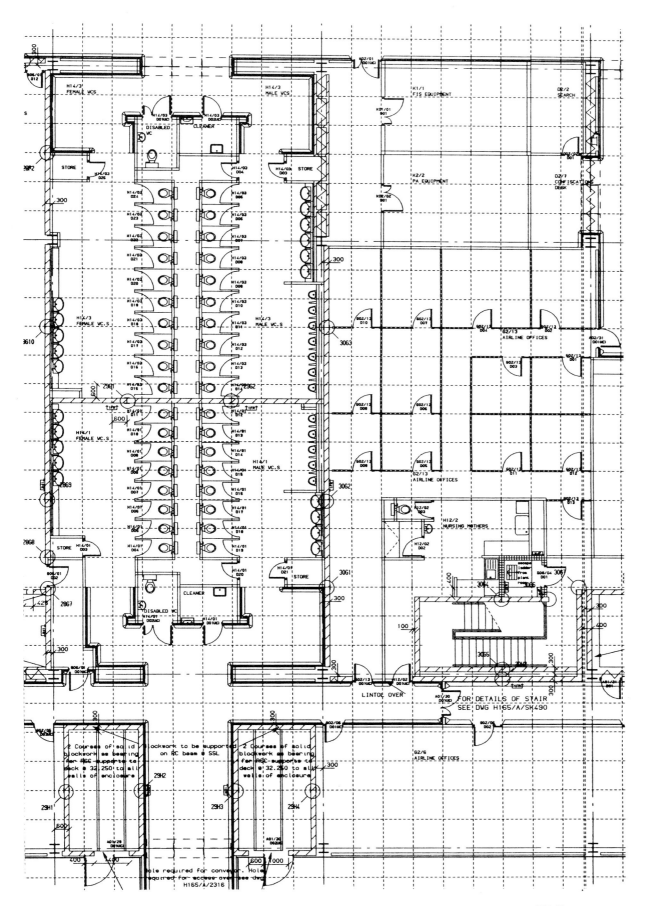

Fig 6.2 GA of a large building: builder's work (Scott Brownrigg and Turner, GDS)

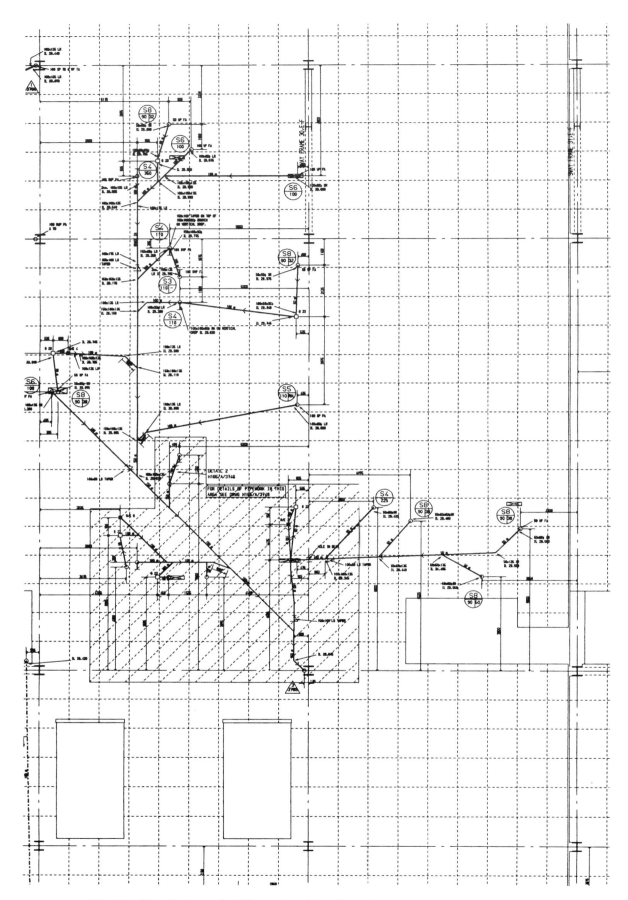

Fig 6.3 GA of a large building: plumbing (Scott Brownrigg and Turner, GDS)

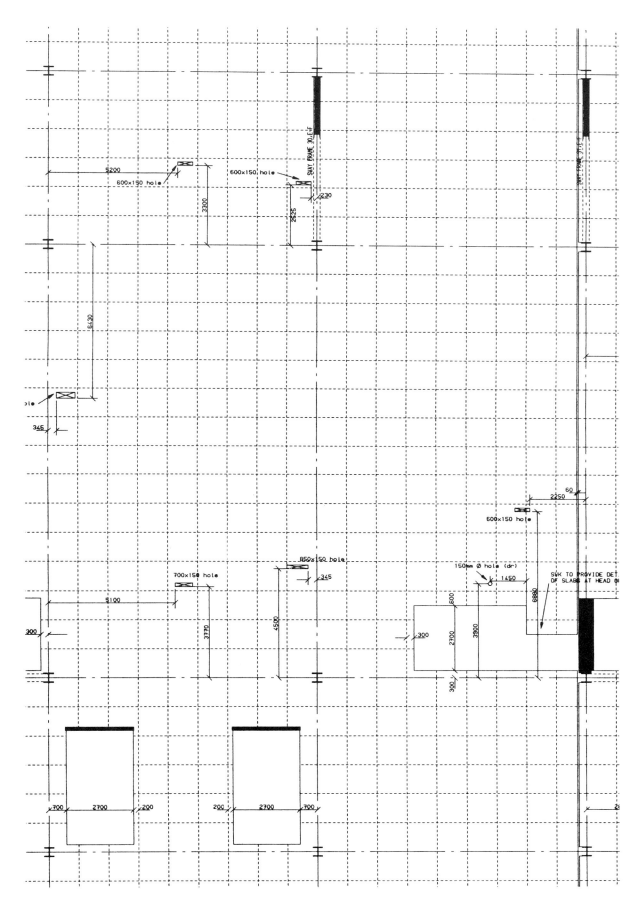

Fig 6.4 GA of a large building: concrete floors (Scott Brownrigg and Turner, GDS)

HEATHROW TERMINAL 4   PACKAGE 755 DOOR SCHEDULE   DRAWING H165/A/64243 SHEET   2

DOOR NUMBER	ROOM NAME	DESCRIPTION	FIRE RATING	NOM. FRAME SIZE	SIDE PANEL SIZE	OVER PANEL SIZE	FRAME PROFILES	MODRIC SET REF	SPECIAL NOTES	REVISION B
G02/04 D01	Airlines offices	Type code 2100x1200LGPR left hand,single swing fixed glazed panel right 2040x774 44mm solid core melamine faced	None	3000 x 1200	2915 x 240 x 44	940 x 774 x 44	Left P1 mid P8 right P5 head P6	P38		
G02/04 D02	Airlines offices	Type code 2100x1200RGPL right hand,single swing fixed glazed panel left 2040x774 44mm solid core melamine faced	None	3000 x 1200	2915 x 240 x 44	940 x 774 x 44	Left P5 mid P8 right P1 head P6	P38		
G02/05 D01	Airlines offices	Type code 2100x1200RGPL right hand,single swing fixed glazed panel left 2040x774 44mm solid core melamine faced	None	3000 x 1200	2915 x 240 x 44	940 x 774 x 44	Left P5 mid P8 right P1 head P6	P38		
G02/05 D02	Airlines offices	Type code 2100x1200LGPR left hand,single swing fixed glazed panel right 2040x774 44mm solid core melamine faced	None	3000 x 1200	2915 x 240 x 44	940 x 774 x 44	Left P1 mid P8 right P5 head P6	P38		

SCOTT BROWNRIGG & TURNER   ARCHITECTS   8 NOV 83

Fig 6.5 Sample door schedule (Scott Brownrigg and Turner, GDS)

everything might prove to be wasteful in design effort. The building designer is well able to think in 3-D and eventually the results of his work must be a series of 2-D drawings for the contractor. It does help, however, if the manufacturer's name or other descriptive material can be attached to graphical components within the computer data model, to facilitate the printing of bills of materials.

It is not possible to generalise too much, however. An exception to the above view occurs when the building is dominated by very highly standardised components, and the component density is high. For example, hospitals with their high services content can fall into this category. If time and trouble is taken to build up a database containing full 3-D descriptions of the range of standard components to be used, the benefits of being able to design in full 3-D may repay the initial effort. The designer can achieve a higher degree of optimisation simply by rearranging components in different ways, and viewing the results from different viewpoints. Figs 6.8 to 6.10 illustrate this. It is cheaper to deal with impractical layouts and clashing of tightly packed components on a screen, compared with making alterations with the actual components later on site.

In other buildings, some architects and structural engineers may prefer to work in 2-D, for simplicity and to achieve high productivity. The services engineer on the other hand is rather more likely to prefer at least some element of the third dimension, whether box geometry or full 3-D. This arises simply because it is the services designer who usually comes along last in the design process. He bears all the responsibility of fitting his services components around or through the existing structure and architectural elements in an unobtrusive and practical arrangement. Figs 6.11 to 6.13 show related plan, section and perspective views of building services which have been generated automatically from the same building data model using the RUCAPS system.

A characteristic of buildings is that there are typically tens of thousands of components,

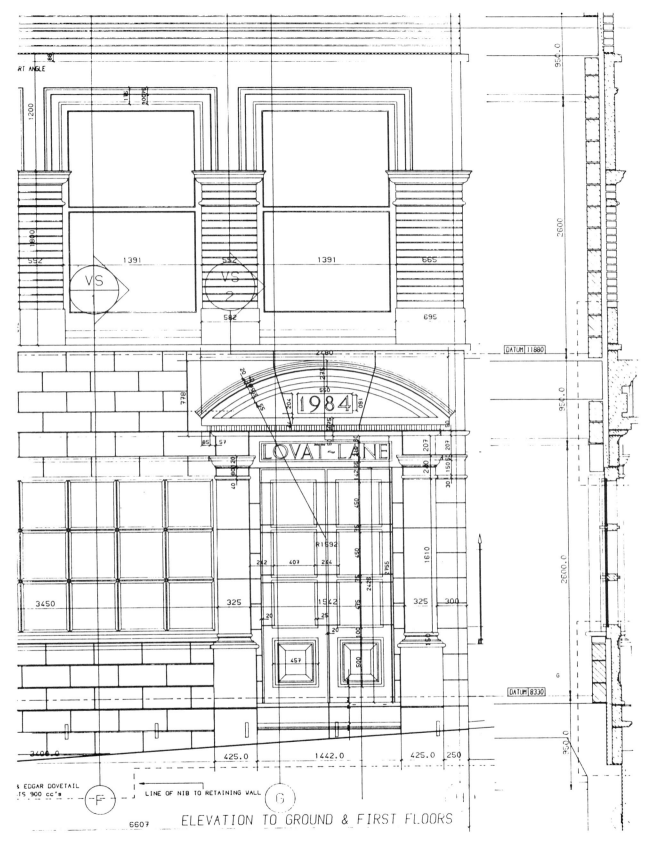

Fig 6.6 Building elevation and section (2-D drawing) (The Thomas Saunders Partnership, GDS)

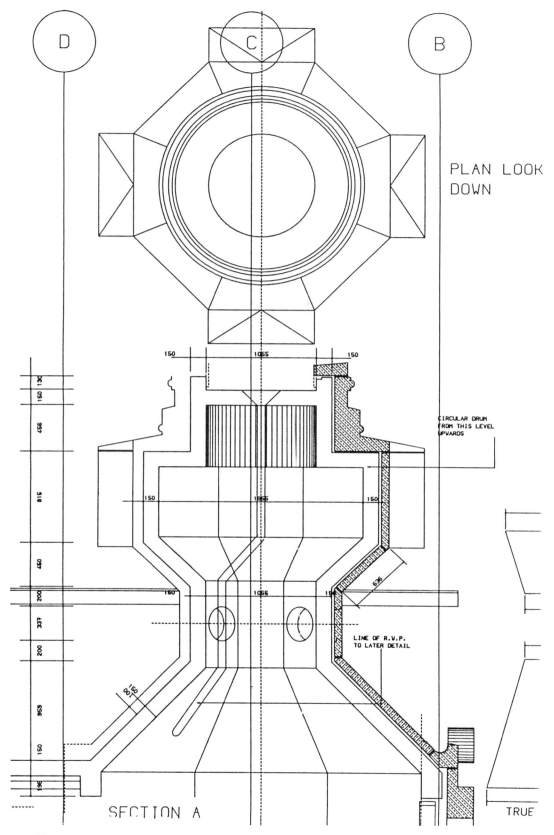

Fig 6.7 Plan and section of stone cupola (The Thomas Saunders Partnership, GDS)

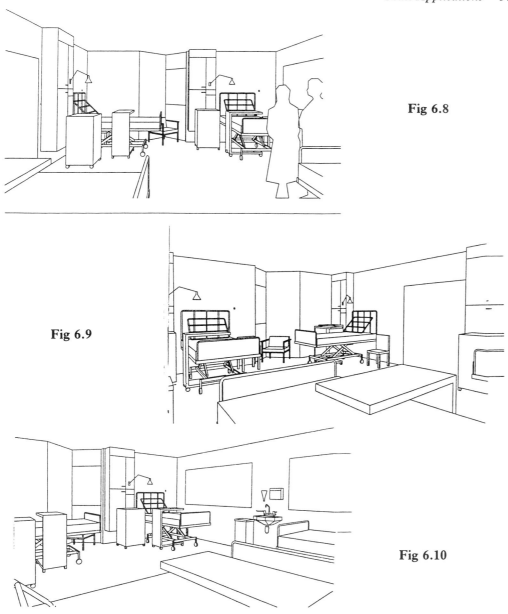

Fig 6.8

Fig 6.9

Fig 6.10

Figs 6.8 to 6.10
Perspective views in a planned hospital ward (North Western Regional Health Authority, ACROPOLIS)

although many are similar items repeated many times over at different locations. So when CAD methods are employed, keys to success are:

Simple representation (frequently symbols are adequate)
Very rapid positioning of components
Accurate positioning of components
Ease of copying components
Ease of moving previously placed components
Use of parameterised shapes, i.e. the same basic components that occur in different sizes, for example, steel sections, pipes, ducts, radiators.

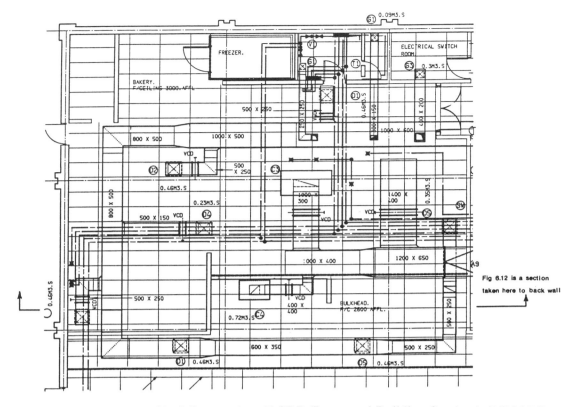

Fig 6.11 Plan view of building services (ACDP (Integrated Building Services), RUCAPS)

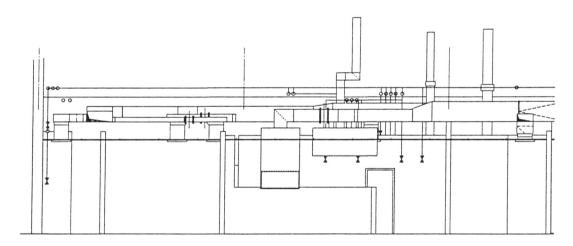

Fig 6.12 Section view of building services (ACDP (Integrated Building Services), RUCAPS)

In some CAD systems the act of copying a component each time involves the duplication of its entire graphical data within the database, as well as storing the new position. In use for building design, such databases rapidly become large, cumbersome and use up much computer power. Systems more suitable for building design would merely store the new component position together with a reference pointer back to the original single set of graphical data. This is much more concise.

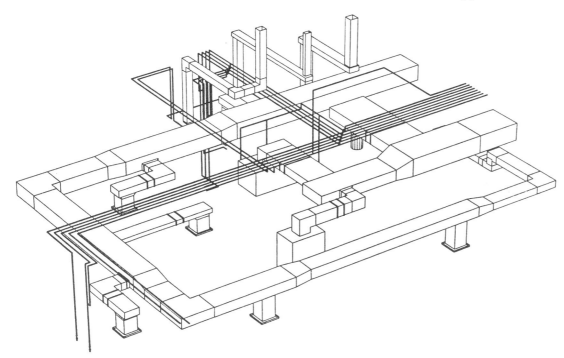

Fig 6.13 Perspective view of building services (ACDP (Integrated Building Services), RUCAPS)

The large number of components and the variety of disciplines makes a sophisticated layering or component selection system very necessary.

When a designer works on a drawing board, he may be working either on a general arrangement at small scale, or on details at large scale. Large components tend to be shown on the general arrangement but the joints between them are on detail drawings. What tends to get missed out in this process, only to reappear as headaches on site, are the problems of fit between different items.

However in CAD operation the concept of drawings and scale tends to remain rather in the background until after the design is basically finished, and the drawing sheets have to be plotted. Before that time it is the data model that rules. In 2-D working this may be an entire floor with all construction and components. In box geometry it is the whole building. So element after element can be placed with considerable precision. If there are large precast concrete cladding panels, then these can be placed side by side with the correct space left for jointing and tolerances. This of course is how it is attempted manually with the GA drawing. But now the designer can zoom in as much as he likes with a screen to explore the problems of fit between unlike components placed perhaps at different times by different designers. So the gulf between general arrangement design and detail design is rather less apparent. This is a major benefit.

Some thought needs to be given to how certain detail will ultimately be presented on drawings. At small scale little may be shown of any item or component apart from an outline. On large scale drawings, more detail may be required. Presentation for each instance can be made easier if the more limited graphics is included in one category or layer, and the greater detail in another. Then the choice for particular drawings can be made simply by the user turning on the relevant categories for each display or plot.

Building product database

Because of the extremely wide variety of a typical design practice's workload, it is not feasible for any one firm to assemble a comprehensive and up-to-date knowledge of all products which it is likely to specify. The design professions are accustomed to requesting and receiving product information free, made available by the manufacturers in the form of data sheets, brochures and catalogues. Firms operating a CAD system are faced with the problem of how to introduce product information into their system so that it is easily available for them to use.

An organisation called Architectural Data Systems Ltd (ADS) has undertaken the task of creating and distributing a building product database. Financed by manufacturers, this service is provided free of charge to CAD users. ADS undertake the input and regular updating of a library of building products in a form compatible with several of the CAD systems now in use. The designer can quickly run through a particular manufacturer's product range, or recommended details, choose an item and then insert the graphics or the specification text into his drawing or project documentation. He can use the data as many times as required. The database already includes the products of several of the leading UK building materials suppliers.

CIVIL ENGINEERING, GROUND MODELLING AND HIGHWAY DESIGN

Drawings required for civil engineering are too varied to allow many generalisations to be made. Many of the points discussed under buildings apply equally in this area. Figs 6.14 and 6.15 are examples of site plans for large community facilities and include tabulated setting-out data. Fig. 6.16 is an example taken from a set of standard drainage details. Fig. 6.17 shows details produced with a special module of the Cambridge Interactive Systems Ltd MEDUSA system. This module deals with the design of ductile iron flanged pipework, including the many standard fittings.

Ground modelling is a technique which has application in many areas of civil engineering. Perhaps it can be illustrated best by reference to the design of highways.

Highway design is essentially a complex geometrical problem. It starts with the requirement to plan a route between two points, and the geometry of the existing ground surface in the area. There will be potential constraints along the route in the form of existing natural or manmade features. Their nature and size will determine whether they are real constraints that have to be avoided, or whether some other provision is possible. Ownership of land is clearly a factor. Any chosen alignment must be satisfactory for the vehicles at whatever design speed is relevant, with minimum radius of curves, maximum gradients and necessary superelevations all being factors. Earth movement forms a large proportion of the cost of most road schemes and the highway engineer will wish to balance the 'cut' and 'fill' after making allowances for bulking or shrinkage of materials. The final road surface must drain freely and effectively. Adequate clearances from structures and other features, and sight lines, must be maintained. Then there will be a relationship between the alignment and the nature and cost of structures such as bridges and retaining walls. Finally, and certainly not least in importance, there is the aesthetics of the design to be considered.

Of course there are other factors, such as the nature of materials available, noise, amenity and so on, but geometry has at least some bearing on most of these too. The complexities are such that it is not too surprising that, until recently, there was little scope for investigating several alternative designs or of optimising any one solution.

However when the computer did become widely available to highway designers some two decades ago, they quickly seized their opportunity and now most roads are designed with its aid. Programs such as BIPS (British Integrated Program System for Highway Design) and MOSS were developed and are now widely used.

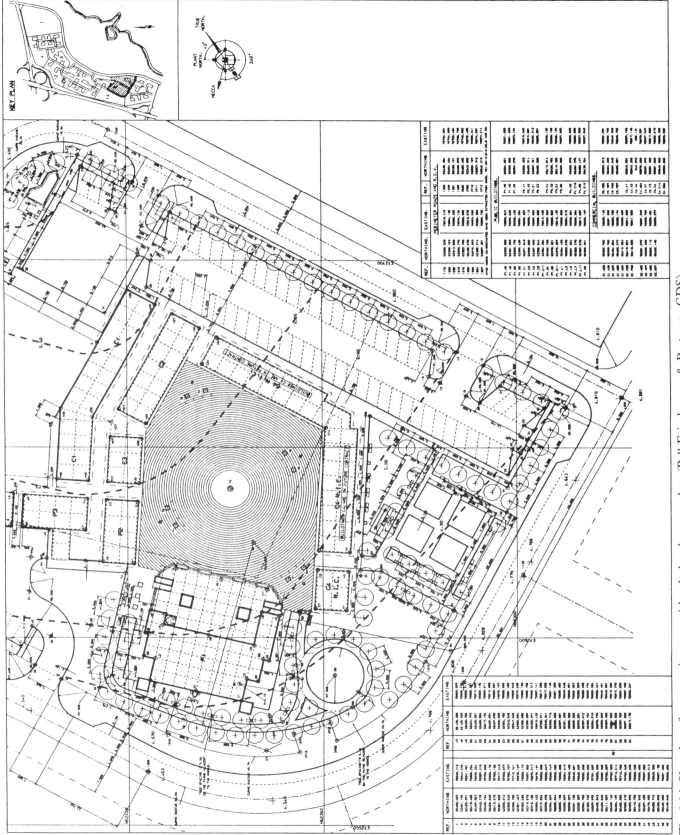

Fig 6.14 Site plan of community area with tabulated survey data (Pell Frischmann & Partners, GDS)

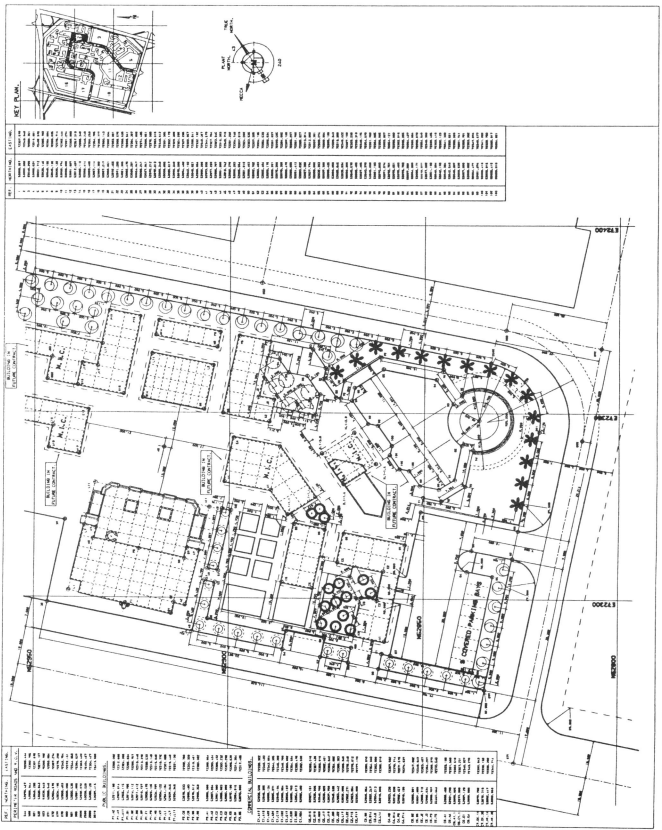

Fig 6.15 Site plan of community area with tabulated survey data (Pell Frischmann & Partners, GDS)

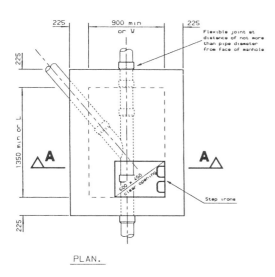

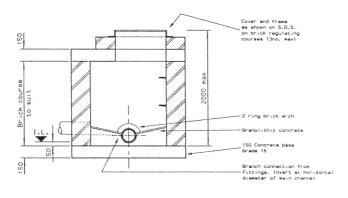

Fig 6.16 Standard drainage detail (IDC Consultants Ltd, GDS)

The use of a DGM (digital ground model) is the basis of these methods. A DGM is simply a data model comprising the three coordinates of a large number of ground points which collectively can define the surface. The points can be on a rectangular, square or triangular grid. The MOSS program uses a 'string' DGM. With this the ground is defined by the three coordinates of ground points along strings. These are lines (not normally straight) in three dimensional space which for example might be features such as the bed of a small stream, a contour line, the top of a railway embankment, or the edge of an existing road.

The level of any other ground point can be estimated automatically by a process of mathematical interpolation between surrounding known points. Accuracy depends on the regularity of the ground surface, the size of mesh or density of strings, and the method of interpolation adopted.

The road designer must define the horizontal and vertical alignment of his road. The programs can assist to some degree because of their ability to perform geometric calculations. Several related programs are now available which can help to optimise the horizontal and vertical alignments. With the alignments and cross-section of the road

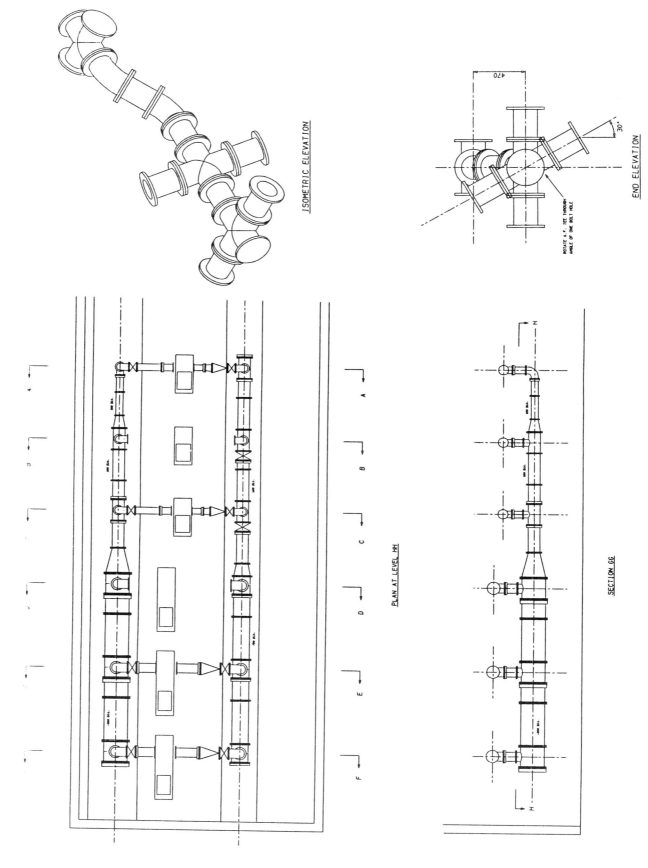

Fig 6.17 Ductile iron flanged pipework details (Severn Trent Water Authority, Soar Division, MEDUSA)

determined, the computer can perform the necessary calculations to determine volumes of cut and fill, mass haul data, and to produce graphical output such as cross-sections, plan views, longitudinal sections and perspective views.

MOSS in particular is not limited in application to highway design, and has been used for general surface modelling, ground surveys, landscaping, airport design and mining. Nevertheless when used for road geometry it is not so flexible that it will allow the structural engineer to add all details of the bridges, retaining walls and other miscellaneous detail.

These programs are not CAD systems in the generally accepted sense. Input is all predefined. The graphical output is automatically generated and cannot be adjusted or added to interactively. But the process has been described because it is an excellent example of a potential application for a highly proficient CAD system. But something more than a general-purpose system is needed, because of the specialist needs of the highway engineer such as mass haul calculations. In the short term the full requirement might be met by using a CAD system in conjunction with MOSS and other programs by providing suitable interfaces for data transfer. Presumably in the longer term either the highway systems will be developed to include CAD facilities, or a CAD system will be developed further to include the specialist procedures needed by the highway engineer.

SITE SURVEYS, MAPPING AND UTILITIES

When a site survey has established the coordinates of the main survey stations, they could be input to the CAD system. Then the geometry of the new project could relate to these. Other features on the site such as existing buildings, roads, hydrants, manholes and so on could be input using the distances and angles from the fixed survey points as recorded by the site surveyor. Site detail can be measured conveniently by tacheometric methods.

The main problem has been with the typing in of all the data and in checking it to eliminate errors. Increasing use is being made by surveyors of electronic theodolites and automatic distance measuring devices as well as data recorders and hand held microcomputers. Some of these can produce data in a form suitable for direct input to larger computers. Survey adjustments can be made and plotted site surveys are produced in this way by survey firms. Where suitable interface programs are available, such site data can be supplied directly from the surveyor to the CAD system via the medium of magnetic tape.

When survey data is available on aerial photographs, then it is possible to capture the data from 3-D views using stereodigitisers. Again with suitable interfaces, these machines can output data in the form of coordinates on magnetic tape, and suitable for direct input to CAD systems. Careful checking of such data is still required. A new kind of stereodigitiser workstation is coming into use which will permit the user to interactively view and check the detail as he is taking it off.

Again with suitable interface programs, existing maps held in digital form can be read into a CAD system to provide the geometrical framework for new projects. For example, some UK Ordnance Survey (OS) plans are held in digital form and can be supplied on magnetic tapes. Unfortunately these are still only available for a small proportion of the country.

These OS maps have traditionally been held on individual sheets, and the digital maps available on tapes perpetuate this approach. It is probable however that the land area of interest in any particular job will spread over more than one sheet. Most systems have not yet developed sufficiently to permit the input of several sheets, and then to allow the user to select and operate on a continuous area which crosses sheet boundaries. Alternatively a system may be able to join perhaps only two but not four sheets or more sheets simultaneously. This would be an unfortunate limitation if, as frequently applies in these cases, the 'action' is at the corner of four sheets! It should also be appreciated that the edges of OS sheets do not match up exactly. If the computer is used to join them, small discontinuities can be apparent in continuous features such as roads, footpaths and administrative area boundaries. Some mapping systems have routines to deal with this problem; otherwise the operators will have to make adjustments themselves.

Much record information held by local authorities and public utilities is held on very old linen maps. It may be necessary to digitise these. Procedures may be needed for transforming the resulting map coordinates from one coordinate system to another. A further complex problem arises because these old maps have themselves inevitably become distorted with time. Even when the map shows an Ordnance grid, this will be distorted and all the data referenced to it will be incorrect. This is a problem which must be addressed. Some mapping packages have sophisticated mathematical routines for rectifying these problems and for giving the best fit result. These routines vary in their accuracy and in their ability to cope with specific problems.

When the site information is safely in the CAD system, and the geometry of the new project is superimposed, it is then possible to extract setting-out data. This is done by indicating the instrument stations and then dimensioning automatically or tabulating the relevant angles, distances or offsets (see fig. 6.18).

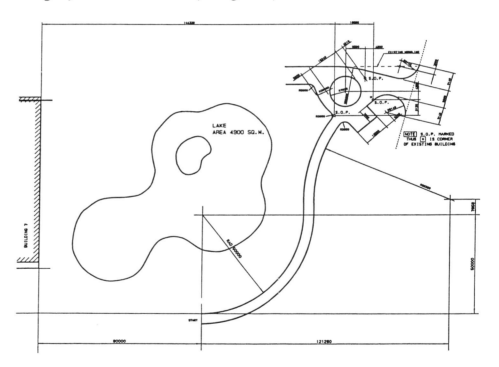

Fig 6.18 Setting-out plan (IDC Consultants Ltd, GDS)

In mapping applications, many of the same CAD techniques that we have already discussed are still relevant. Mention has already been made of the importance of non-graphic databases, of overlaying of different categories of information, and of course of the ability to manipulate and edit large volumes of graphical information. There are other specialist techniques needed. An example is the ability to automatically modify symbology depending on the scale of representation. For the design of modifications to distribution systems, it is useful to be able to automatically make a trace through a complex network.

The precision with which the computer holds and manipulates the basic coordinates is important. For most mapping applications, this needs to be to an accuracy of nine significant figures or better. This is more than most CAD systems can cope with.

In every modern city, it is a major problem to just maintain records of its infrastructure. There are records needed for built form, for land and property ownership, street furniture, and for all the utilities including gas, electricity, water, drainage, telephone, cable television and traffic signalling. New buildings are constantly being erected, old ones discarded, and always new and better services are being installed. It is indeed a dynamic environment with every service interacting in a complex manner with others. Every time a hole is dug in a city street, or any new service provided, it is necessary to make cross-checks with all the other authorities. It is a very time consuming, labour intensive and error prone business.

As the cost of computer graphics continues to fall, it seems likely that CAD will play an increasing role in maintaining these records in the future. The application is restricted, however, by the difficulty of transferring the huge volume of existing information from old maps and plans to the computer. Even when this is achieved, the quality of the information only matches what is already available in the current form. However the speed at which it may be accessed, and the ability to modify and add to it, is likely to be greatly enhanced. So it seems that over an extended period, the quality of these vital records could be gradually improved by computer techniques.

Some public utility authorities are already using CAD systems and gaining experience. What they need is an ability to manipulate huge graphical databases, with high precision, and linkages with large non-graphic databases. It is not sufficient merely to know the line taken by a pipe. Ideally what they would like is the information that it is a 200 mm ductile iron water pipe laid in 1974, plus its invert levels and an identification code for each particular run of pipe. For each manhole in a drainage system, a record of its type, material, size, year of construction, depth and an identification code is required in addition to its exact location. Often this information is not even known at present, but as isolated discoveries of information are made, there needs to be a quick and easy means of adding it to a database.

The need for a degree of cooperation between the different authorities is evident. When there is a burst water main in the city, somebody needs to know the location and details of any other services in the vicinity, and they need it rapidly. Ultimately this cooperation could amount to connections between individual databases to permit one authority to examine and use – but not to alter – data held by another. But with problems of compatibility of systems and equipment, this is still a long way off. In the shorter term transfers of information between some systems might be possible at intervals using magnetic tape.

Abilities to maintain vast stores of records, and to communicate the selected information rapidly to those that need it, are the keys. Increasingly public utility authorities are finding it difficult or almost impossible to keep up when traditional manual methods are used. With the proliferation of projects even within one organisation, it sometimes happens that operatives arrive on one job and are unaware of another team working on another job which interacts with theirs. Holding information in one place will eventually be an answer. The output of the most up-to-date information to microfilm for display on reading devices installed in field trucks is being tried with some success.

REINFORCED CONCRETE DETAILING

A reinforced concrete structure is usually planned in two separate phases. The first is the design phase performed by the engineer. He chooses the structural form and reasonable member sizes, and then analyses the proposed structure. He calculates the amount of reinforcement required at key points in the more important members. If the results are not to his satisfaction, he has to change the structure and reanalyse it until a suitable structure is determined.

The engineer is normally responsible also for the drawings which show the general arrangement and outlines of the structure. These drawings and the calculation results are handed over for the second phase, the detailing.

In some countries, including the UK, the design organisation may be a consulting engineer, a government body, a local authority or the design department of a large company. The two phases are normally carried out by the one organisation, and often but not always by different people within it. Sometimes the detailing is done by a specialist outside firm, but under the direct control of the designer. In some other countries, the engineer produces typical details only, and the bulk of the detailing is done by the successful contractor or steel supplier, and approved by the engineer. The detailing phase involves the production of reinforcement detail drawings and bar schedules.

Computers and concrete detailing

The simplest programs used in the past have performed the scheduling function only. The dimensions and other information for each bar group were input, and the computer checked that the shape conformed with national standards and good detailing practice. The total length of each bar was calculated and the bars were sorted into those for similar structural elements, and into steel types, bar shapes and length ranges. The output was a bar schedule and weight schedule for costing purposes. Although undoubtedly useful, there was much input for comparatively little processing.

A somewhat more ambitious approach is taken by many other programs that can be used to detail particular concrete elements. Starting with member geometry, material properties and reinforcement required at critical points, these programs determine the numbers and shapes of all the bars required. Then they proceed to schedule the steel. So these programs take over the detailer's role within the limited orbit of the particular type of structural element. Such programs can only solve problems where the basis of decision making can be anticipated by the original program writer. They are relevant for such elements as precast concrete units, straightforward beams, columns and slabs. But complex or special elements are not covered, and these programs often have difficulties at the structural junctions with other members. The BARD system produced by the UK Cement & Concrete Association follows a rather similar principle and the output includes plotted reinforcing drawings of the element.

Certain programs exist which start off with the engineer's description of the structure, material properties and loading. These perform a structural analysis and then proceed to automatically calculate bar shapes, sizes, and numbers. The output comprises bar schedules, weight schedules, and fixing schedules. The last make reference to standard preprinted drawings and the tabulation for each group of bars indicates exactly where it is to be placed in the structure. Programs such as this are necessarily very complex and have to incorporate all the logic for detailing the particular structural type. Among the better known examples was the GENESYS reinforced concrete building system produced by the Property Services Agency of the UK government.

These then are the conventional methods of computer detailing. The drawbacks can be summarised as follows:

1 They can deal with relatively straightforward concrete elements only. They leave the difficult cases to the detailer. He gets little practice at simple detailing to prepare him

for the difficult problems. There is less creative work for him to do and many detailers are reduced to mere form fillers for much of their time.

2 For the site staff, the graphical output is often in unfamiliar format and is a poor substitute for the conventional true-to-scale reinforcing drawing. Worse still, a typical project may be partly detailed by computer with one form of drawings, and partly by hand with conventional drawings.

3 The programs have to tackle member junctions in a predetermined and inflexible manner. They may insert additional loose splice bars at member intersections. This simplifies the program but may well use more steel and creates more congestion of reinforcement at critical places. It is wrong to make small savings in design costs if the increase in construction costs is larger.

4 It is not easy to amend the computer output manually.

After two decades of development, the result is that computer detailing is still only adopted on a fairly limited scale, even though there is a serious lack of skilled detailers.

CAD for concrete detailing

What seems to have been forgotten too often is that detailing itself, especially the choice and positioning of bars, is creative work. The normal detailer can usually produce a better result than his computer programming colleagues in most given circumstances. What he needs is a tool to help with the routine parts of the process, allowing him to give his full attention to the creative element of his work. The interactive graphics approach with the detailer in control would allow him to bring all his experience to bear on the most difficult, specialist or unfamiliar detailing problems. These would include the complicated member joints where congestion of steel and clashing of bars are potential problems.

Using a normal 2-D CAD system, concrete outlines can be copied within seconds from previously prepared structural general arrangement drawings. Under the control of a detailer the system could then be used to create reinforcement detail drawings, and indeed these could have the appearance of the traditional product.

When this is tried in practice, however, the intricacies involved in the input of bar shapes, their placing and the specialised annotation all combine to make the economics of the operation somewhat marginal. The standard CAD system is also incapable of creating bar schedules in their accepted format. So, some extra facilities must be provided for the concrete detailer, and these in practice would probably take the form of a specialist CAD package. The RCDS (reinforced concrete detailing system) produced by Applied Research of Cambridge is one such package, and it is now described.

RCDS – reinforced concrete detailing system

This is integrated with the GDS system described in chapter 5. RCDS is for interactive detailing, conforms with the recommendations of BS4466:1981, and is used after the design calculations have been completed. In the control of the detailer its functions are first to draw and annotate the bars on the reinforcement drawings, and secondly to create the bar and weight schedules automatically.

Built into RCDS is an understanding of bar shape codes. The detailer can select a bar shape, and set it down in the structure in whatever location he wishes. So he has complete flexibility to detail any structure, such as bridge decks, grain silos, or arch dams – however simple or complex.

The general arrangement and concrete outlines can be drawn with GDS – the general-purpose draughting system. The detailer takes over and has access to these outline drawings. So he can copy any outlines and features for his own detail drawings. Working from the design calculations and using his own experience, he can start placing bars with RCDS.

For each bar group he defines such items as the steel grade, bar size and the group reference or 'mark number'. The geometry of any bar can be defined by its shape code and the dimensions of each leg. These lengths can be typed in explicitly, but more commonly the detailer would specify each dimension simply by indicating two points on the screen. Fig. 6.19 shows how this might be done in practice with a shape code 35 bar. This is a straight bar with a standard bend at each end. So one dimension only is needed to define it exactly. The detailer 'hits' the two points on the concrete outline and gives a negative correction for cover and tolerance.

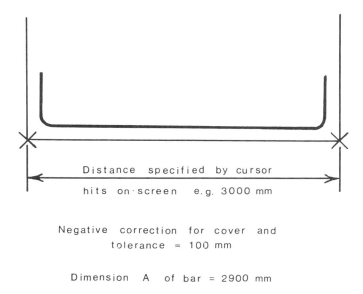

Fig 6.19 Definition of reinforcing bar geometry: shape code 35 bar

Another example is shown in fig. 6.20. Here bar 1 was defined previously, and bar 2 is to be placed so as to lap with it. The length of bar 2 could be defined by the two 'hits' shown, but this time the correction would be positive and equal to the desired lap length, less one cover distance. The total lengths of bent bars are calculated by the computer. Leg lengths are rounded to 5 mm and total lengths to 25 mm as required by BS4466.

Warning messages inform the detailer if he has violated specification requirements or certain rules of good detailing practice built into the system.

Now the sized bar can be 'placed' by the detailer. Using commands, he can rotate it or hand it to get it into its correct orientation, and then set it down in its correct position relative to the concrete outline. The computer then has all the information necessary to draw the bar accurately, even with the bends drawn to scale. By choice of command he can draw other views of the same bar, when it would appear either as a straight line, or in section as a small circle. One frequently used command enables a row of bars to be drawn in section as a row of equally spaced 'dots'. Commands can be entered by keyboard or more conveniently using a menu on a data tablet.

Bar tagging is the means of indicating the extent of a group of bars when only one or perhaps two bars are drawn fully. This is done with the pattern of arrows and lines shown in fig. 6.21. The TAG command is used by pointing to a bar already drawn, and then with the screen cursor the limits of the group are marked out. The graphics are then generated and displayed automatically.

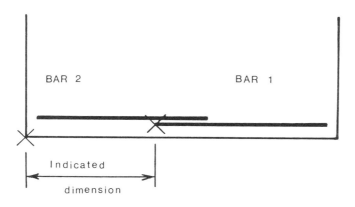

BAR 2   BAR 1

Indicated

dimension

Correction = Lap length - Cover distance

Fig 6.20 Definition of reinforcing bar geometry: lapping bars

The definition and drawing of the bars have now been explained. The next step is bar annotation. Any bar might be shown on several views, but by convention only one view is fully annotated with:

The grade of steel, size of bar and mark number
The number of bars in the group
Bar spacing and/or other text, e.g. T or NF to indicate layer.

A command is available for this annotation. The detailer has merely to point at the bar and supply the missing information – the number of bars and the text. The annotation block is generated and placed at a position indicated by the detailer, and an arrowed leader line pointing to the bar is generated automatically (see fig. 6.22). In other views, only the mark number is needed as annotation.

There are facilities for interrogation of the drawing. Clear gaps between bars, areas of steel or percentage of reinforcement contained in any indicated area are all possibilities.

A typical drawing is built up from individual views of concrete members. Any such view would comprise the concrete outlines, the bars, tagging, annotation, and any other details needed such as waterstops. Facilities exist for the moving of whole views about a drawing, for copying views or for transferring them from one drawing to another. Editing commands enable one view to be created by copying and adapting another view. One example to demonstrate the usefulness of this feature is in the drawing of a concrete floor slab. After one view of one bay is completed, it can be copied and adapted to form views of other similar, but not identical, bays.

Line thicknesses and the size of circles to represent bars in section are automatically selected taking into account bar size and scale. Normally, of course, any bar is represented by a single line, but at scales of say 1:10 they may be represented by double lines which are correctly spaced and radiused. This is a powerful facility for investigating and drawing patterns where the steel is particularly congested.

At any time, a bar schedule can be generated for any member or for the whole drawing. The format conforms with the requirements of BS4466. Where there is missing information, this will be listed on an exception report. A weight schedule lists the total weight of steel in one or several drawings. Bars are sorted into steel grades, bar sizes, and concrete members. Bent bars, binders and straight bars are also separated out. Two

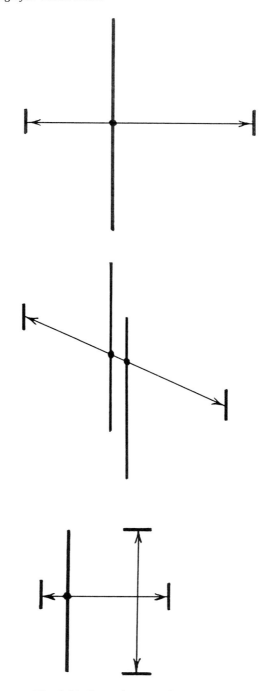

Fig 6.21 Some bar tagging patterns

examples of drawing details created with RCDS are included as figs 6.23 and 6.24. A related bar schedule is shown in fig. 6.25.

Drawing revision control

The ability to create schedules automatically is a major benefit of a system like this. The detailer can have some confidence that the schedule will conform exactly with the current drawing. If a drawing is revised, a correctly revised schedule can be printed automatically.

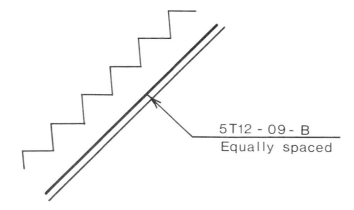

Fig 6.22 Example of bar annotation

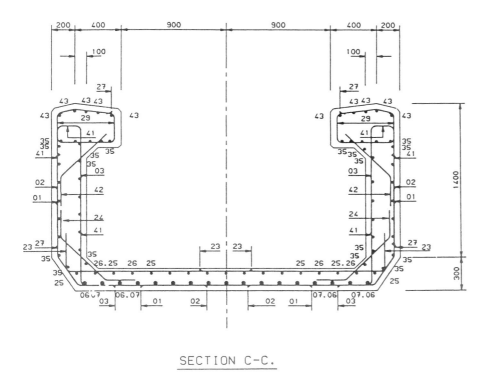

SECTION C-C.

Fig 6.23 RC detail created with RCDS (R. Travers Morgan & Partners, RCDS)

As with all scheduling, however, one major danger is always present. This is simply that the drawing might be amended and then issued with an out-of-date schedule (on separate sheets of paper). If it is not completely clear to all concerned that the schedules and drawing no longer conform, they may be issued and then errors will occur on site.

RCDS has special facilities to help to prevent this happening. When a drawing is being created in the first place, it is in the 'amended' state. Any schedule printed during this time is automatically marked 'provisional'. When a drawing is completed and a bar schedule has been printed with no missing data, i.e. no exception report is produced, then the drawing state automatically changes to 'printed'. Printed schedules are no longer marked as provisional copies. By issuing a command, the detailer would change the drawing state

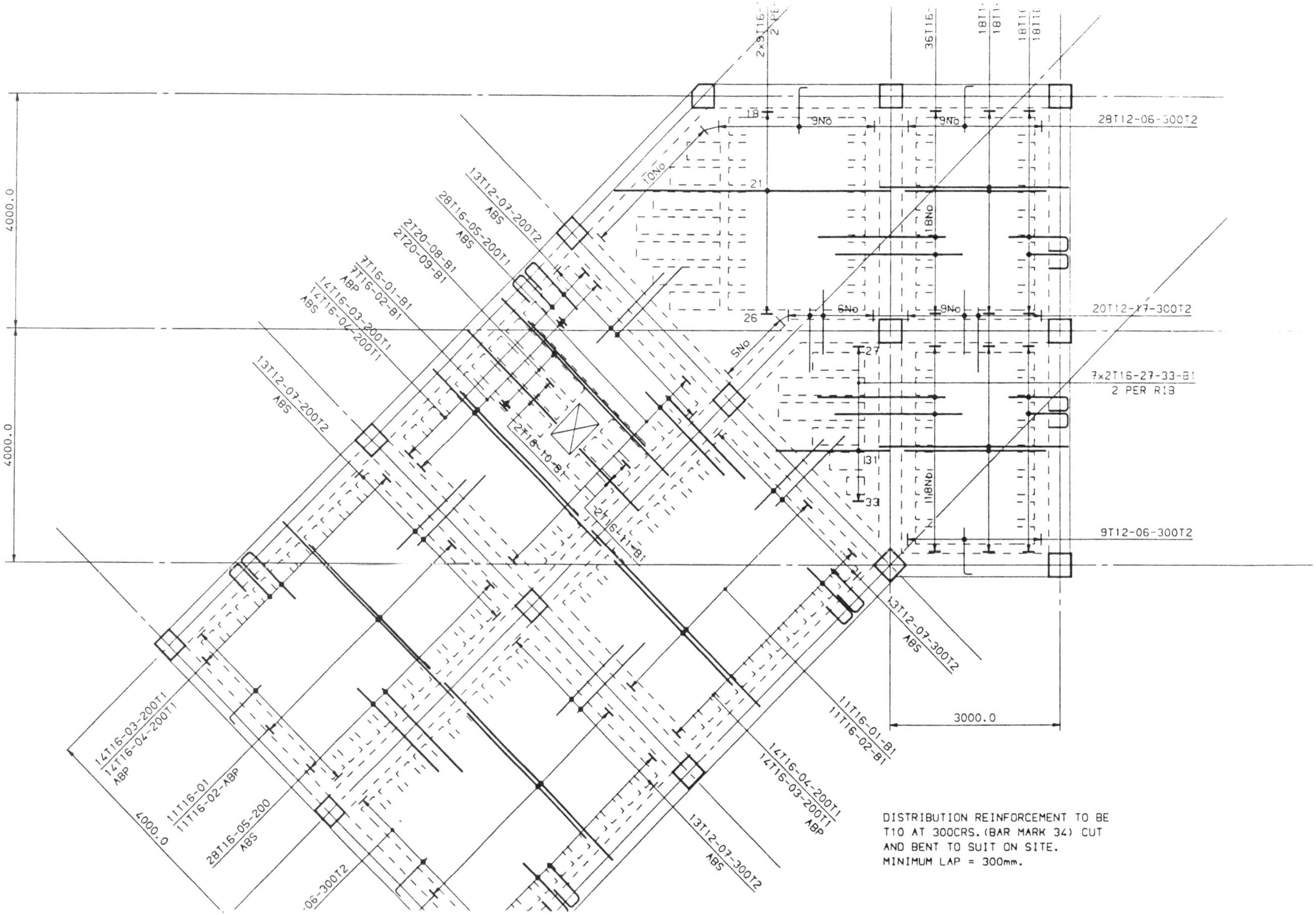

Fig 6.24 RC floor slabs (R. Travers Morgan & Partners, RCDS)

```
                                                            Rev letter
RTM                              Bar Schedule Ref: 003  01

Site ref:                        Date prepared:           Revised:

                                 Prepared by.             Checked by.

-------------------------------------------------------------------------------
         Bar  Type No.  No.of Total Length Shape  *     *     *     *     *
Member   mark and  of   bars  no.   of each code   A     B     C     D     E/r
         size mbrs in               bar £
                   each                mm                 mm    mm    mm    mm
-------------------------------------------------------------------------------

SLAB1    01  T16  1    40    40    4250    20   (4250)
         02  T16  1    40    40    3000    20   (3000)
         03  T16  1    56    56    1775    38    1150   250   (450)
         04  T16  1    56    56    1475    38     850   250   (450)
         05  T16  1    56    56    2000    20   (2000)
         06  T12  1    63    63     925    37     150   (800)
         07  T12  1    52    52    1700    20   (1700)
         08  T20  1     2     2    4250    20   (4250)
         09  T20  1     2     2    3000    20   (3000)
         10  T16  1     2     2    2250    20   (2250)
         11  T16  1     2     2    1500    20   (1500)
         12  T16  1    18    18    3350    20   (3350)
         13  T16  1    18    18    2500    20   (2500)
         14  T16  1    18    18    1575    38    1050   250   (350)
         15  T16  1    18    18    1275    38     750   250   (350)
         16  T16  1    36    36    2250    20   (2250)
         17  T12  1    20    20    1100    20   (1100)
         18  T16  1     2     2    3600    20   (3600)
         19  T16  1     2     2    4000    20   (4000)
         20  T16  1     2     2    4400    20   (4400)
         21  T16  1     2     2    4900    20   (4900)
         22  T16  1     2     2    5300    20   (5300)
         23  T16  1     2     2    5500    20   (5500)
         24  T16  1     2     2    5100    20   (5100)
         25  T16  1     2     2    4700    20   (4700)
         26  T16  1     2     2    4300    20   (4300)
         27  T16  1     2     2    1900    20   (1900)
         28  T16  1     2     2    2400    20   (2400)
         29  T16  1     2     2    2800    20   (2800)
         30  T16  1     2     2    2500    20   (2500)
         31  T16  1     2     2    2000    20   (2000)
         32  T16  1     2     2    1600    20   (1600)
         33  T16  1     2     2    1200    20   (1200)
         34  T10                    360    20   RANDOM LENGTH
                                   metres       CUT TO SUIT ON SITE

-------------------------------------------------------------------------------
 * Rounded to nearest 5mm.  £ Rounded to nearest  25mm
```

Fig 6.25 Bar schedule (R. Travers Morgan & Partners, RCDS)

to 'locked' at the time when he issues the drawing and associated schedules. After this time, no alterations can be made to the drawing, unless he deliberately initiates a drawing revision.

To revise a drawing, he must use a command to formally 'unlock' the drawing. When any changes are in fact made, the drawing reverts to the 'amended' state, and the drawing number is automatically altered with a revision letter A, B etc. When a bar schedule is next printed, all the additions, deletions and changes will be marked on this with the appropriate drawing revision letter. The schedules will be marked 'provisional' if there are any exceptions, and so on as before.

With this form of drawing revision control, the detailer can be more confident that his schedules will accurately conform with the drawings, and errors are much less likely to be made by anyone concerned.

A CAD-oriented detailing system such as this does not force any particular solutions to be adopted. The detailer is encouraged to make full use of his creative detailing skills to specify bars where and how he sees fit, and thereby to overcome any problems in any type of structure.

STRUCTURAL STEEL DETAILING

Many of the points made already about concrete detailing apply with equal force to the detailing of steel structures. Of course, most steel structures are fabricated from standard sections including the familiar beams, columns, angles, tees, plates, rectangular and circular hollow sections. However, compound members can be built up from such standard elements.

The aim of the designer is to create general arrangement drawings and detail drawings which show the members, joints and fittings with sufficient detail, dimensions and annotation to enable the structure to be fabricated and assembled. He may also need schedules which list the components with their sizes, weights and costs.

An organisation responsible for detailing and fabricating the structure will have the same basic needs, but may place more emphasis on the scheduling. It may in addition require full size templates, saw and drill line charts or numerical control tapes for automatic control of sawing, drilling, welding and other machines.

An outline of how a specialised CAD steel detailing system might work now follows. It must provide facilities for:

1 Automatic generation of members
2 A means of dealing with connection details
3 Scheduling.

Member generation

The system would need to keep details of all the standard sections in a library. Then any one section could be selected with the aid of nested menus. The user first picks off the section type, such as beam, column or angle, and then the nominal size and, where there is still a choice, the appropriate section by weight.

Some means of indicating the length and the location of the member within the structure is needed. This is akin to the dimensioning and positioning of reinforcing bars. In an ideal system, a flexible and simple procedure would allow the detailer to select the view required – a plan or an elevation. This action would cause the view of the member, initially having an arbitrary length, to appear in a corner of the screen. This view could be picked up using the screen cursor by a point at one end of the view, then dragged into position and connected to the structure at this point. Then a point at the other end of the member could be picked up. Like an elastic band, the member could be stretched and connected to another point of the structure.

With interactive facilities such as these, a drawing of the structure could be quickly and accurately 'fabricated' from any basic components. Clearly means are necessary for modifying the end shapes of members from the simple square cut, and for adding items such as stiffeners.

Section views of members, such as columns in plan, could be called up and then dragged across the screen and rotated as necessary until they are in their correct locations.

Connections

The major part of the total cost of any steel structure lies in the connections. This is also where most of the design costs are. A basic problem with steel connections is that there is an almost infinite variety of arrangements possible. Nevertheless, whether computers are involved in the detailing or not, it is always worth while to keep the connections simple and to apply as much standardisation as possible. Most emphasis is now on shop welding and site bolting.

With CAD, there is scope for using a library of standard connection details. Preferably these need to be in parameterised form, so that a detail can be extracted and then easily sized to suit the members to be connected. So library details would be required for end plates, haunched end plates, flange cleats, web cleats, fin plates, top and bottom tees, and so on. Clearly these must conform with the latest and best industry practice. The basic ability of certain CAD systems to allow details to be extracted from libraries and then adapted to suit local conditions is therefore the key to better detailing and better structures. It is also important for an organisation to be able to add new details to this library. Then a fund of useful knowledge and expertise can be accumulated for the future benefit of the organisation.

Facilities are needed for setting out patterns of bolts, and the library must contain elements such as bolts, and symbols for welding and other purposes.

Systems must permit the user to interactively add holes, trimmings and stiffeners to members and to connection elements. Specialist systems may automatically check that elements conform to national or other specifications or standards, for example to check that edge distances from holes are adequate.

Scheduling

Systems that can cope with non-graphic data can hold all information associated with the members and connections used. Designers could then create bills of materials which list the members, sections, lengths, weights and costs. Lists of connections, bolt lists and weld schedules are similarly possible. Paint schedules are easily created. These would draw upon data such as the perimeter of sections and member lengths for the determination of painting areas. With painting specifications and unit costs known, these schedules could also include costs.

A steel fabricator may in addition be interested in sorting such schedules into section sizes and lengths, and in submitting such information into his stockyard management systems.

Two dimensions or three?

At first sight, steel detailing is a good application for full 3-D treatment. The sections are mostly standardised and predetermined, and only a length may be required to describe a member as a three-dimensional object. Members would have to be positioned accurately in 3-D space, however, and this is much more time consuming for the operator. Connections are a problem to describe in full 3-D terms but, where there is a need for only a restricted range of connection types, these could be created once and held in a library. Clearly some facilities for parameterisation of 3-D elements would be a useful feature.

The advantage of 3-D working is that plans, elevations, sections, and isometric or perspective views of the structure could all be generated, perhaps with hidden line removal, from the one basic model. Advanced systems might be capable of detecting clashing of members, and might check on the possibility of bolt fouling, and on insertability and tightenability of bolts.

Organisations engaged in the design of a fairly limited range of complex or costly structures, and which can adopt a somewhat limited range of connection details, may prefer a 3-D system. In these circumstances it is worth while to invest effort in creating the 3-D library. It is also worth expending more resources – in terms of program complexity, operator effort and computer power – to gain the additional benefits that can come from 3-D working. Where a wide variety of work is undertaken, it may be more practical to adopt the 2-D procedure.

PLANT DESIGN

Process plants and other large scale fabrications have become so complex that design by conventional means has become extremely difficult. Models using plastic components have had to be constructed in the past in order to design the dense assemblage of structure, pipes, valves, tanks, instruments and so on. Now several of the larger fabricators have employed CAD systems. These can assist in all phases – schematic planning, analysis, detail design of layout, procurement of materials and components, construction and operation.

One specialist CAD system in this field is PDMS (plant design management system) which is marketed by Prime Computers. The initial phase of scheme design is essentially the build-up of piping and instrumentation diagrams (P&IDs). These are 2-D drawings comprising standard symbols and orthogonal lines to represent pipe connections. Flow diagrams and data sheets are also produced early on.

Then comes the creation of the 3-D model from assemblages of primitive shapes and predefined components including standard pipe shapes, racks and so on. As with most CAD systems, it is easy to make modifications and so to achieve some degree of optimisation. Pipes and supporting structures can be viewed from any angle and the accuracy of dimensions displayed is to within 1 mm regardless of plant size. The system works internally to much greater accuracy still. Such high accuracy in the design makes it much easier to plan, fabricate and incorporate on site the large premanufactured subassemblies. In PDMS there are comprehensive facilities for clash checking. The system can provide warnings of 'hard' clashes between components including structure, pipes, and insulation if present. Alternatively it can warn of 'soft clashes', these being situations where inadequate operational or maintenance space is provided for valve wheels and similar items. Checking on consistency of bore and matching of connection types between adjacent pipes is also possible. There are interfaces to stress analysis programs.

Hidden line removal in views is essential for comprehension of the layout of complex plants. Perspective and isometric views are frequently used for construction purposes, although the more familiar plans, elevations and sections are also obtainable. For construction purposes, PDMS can be used for the production of large numbers of stretched isometric drawings. An example of one of these is shown in fig. 6.26, and a view of a large section of a plant is given in fig. 6.27.

Construction is also facilitated by comprehensive scheduling of materials and components. Status of items can be determined, e.g. 'ordered' or 'delivered'. On-site graphics terminals can be used for detailed inspections of the model to resolve construction difficulties. These can also be used to create as-built drawings for plant records, or even for purposes of operation and maintenance of the plant.

Reference has been made to Prime's PDMS system, but other CAD companies that are active in this field include Intergraph and Computervision.

VISUAL IMPACT OF PROJECTS ON ENVIRONMENT

Architects and others need to predict how new construction projects will blend into the existing landscape with the least adverse, or the greatest beneficial, visual impact. Proposals for major projects like power stations, oil refineries, new harbours, roads and tall buildings all attract intensive local or even national interest, and rightly so. This, however, can result in politicians, the public and designers all being involved in debate and in lengthy public enquiries. Of course artists' impressions are produced and expert opinions expressed, but prediction of altered landscapes is often insufficient and inaccurate. This leads to endless argument.

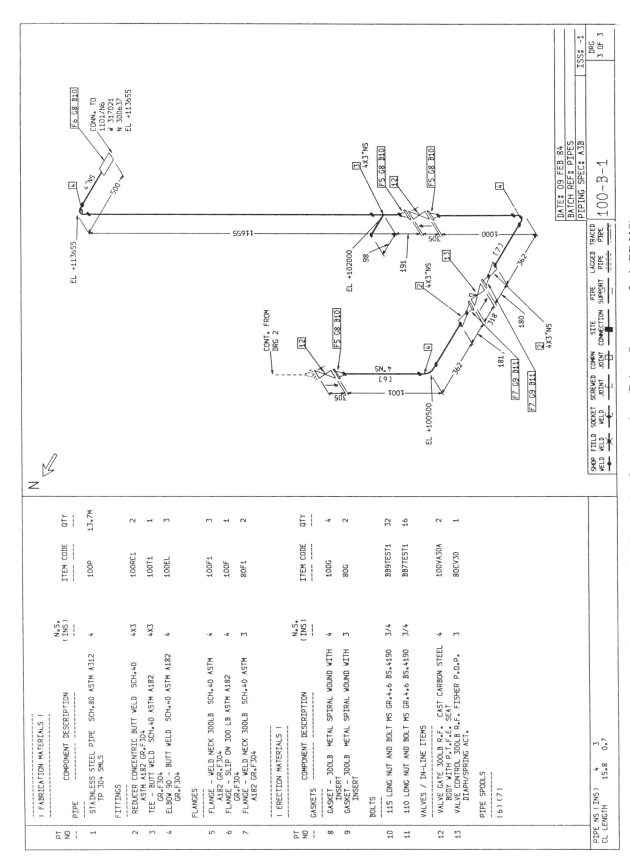

Fig 6.26 Stretched isometric of process plant (Prime Computers Ltd, PDMS)

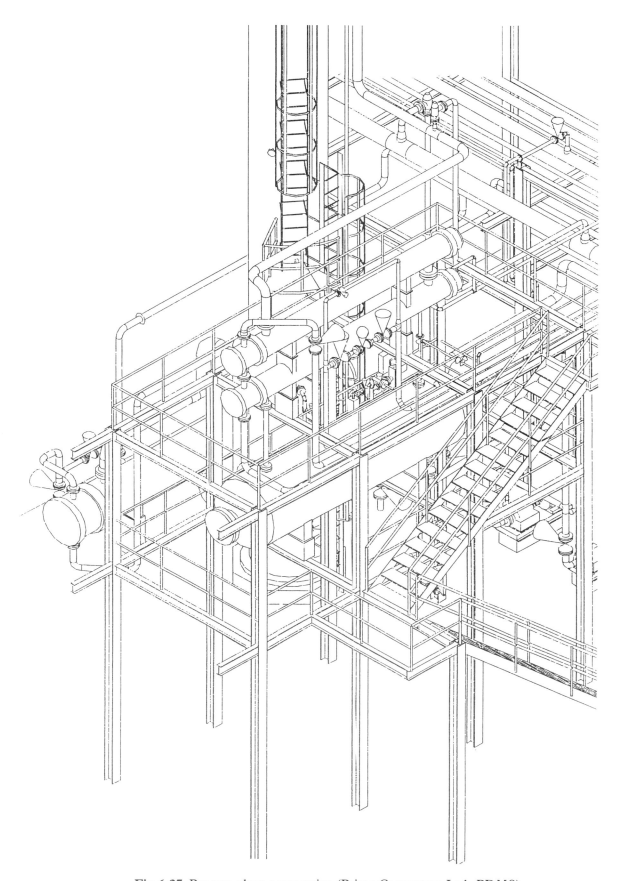

Fig 6.27 Process plant perspective (Prime Computers Ltd, PDMS)

Fig 6.28 Computer perspective view merged with photograph of landscape (ABACUS, Dept of Architecture, Strathclyde University)

Fig 6.29 Photograph of actual building for comparison (ABACUS, Dept of Architecture, Strathclyde University)

Colour computer graphics are now fast reaching the stage where realistic views of proposed projects can be created. Such views can be integrated with views of the existing landscape in which they will be located. Professional designers and the public at large can then benefit from a greater appreciation of the proposals themselves, and of the alternatives. These can literally be viewed from all angles. Constructive criticism can be accommodated and more rapidly investigated.

These methods, sometimes referred to as 'visual impact analysis', have been studied by the ABACUS unit of the Department of Architecture at the University of Strathclyde with the aid of programs such as Bible and Vista. The latter is a 3-D colour perspective package with hidden line removal. With this it is possible to create coloured, textured and shaded perspectives of the project itself from a data model. It requires to know the colour of the various surfaces, and the positions of the viewer and of the sun so that shadows can be calculated.

It is also possible to create 3-D views of the landscape from any position using a digital ground model and a suitable program. These procedures have been developed by Design Innovations Research in Edinburgh. Practical difficulties lie in the accurate visual representation of superficial features such as trees, crops, and existing buildings. An alternative is to photograph the landscape and to superimpose on this the computer produced view of the project by photomontage techniques. The problem remains of how to effectively slip the computer view in behind relevant foreground. However this can be done with the use of colour transparencies of the site overlaid on computer views of the project with some editing. Then the result is rephotographed on a light table. This subject has been studied by C. Purdie (Computer-aided visual impact analysis, PhD Thesis, University of Strathclyde, 1983). Fig. 6.28 is a view of a building created from a computer model merged in this way with photographs of the landscape. For comparison, fig.6.29 is a photograph showing the actual building in its setting.

Of course the human artist can intervene to improve final products. However the realism of automatically created views is being improved all the time. For example, studies are being made into the representation of different building materials such as brick, into surface texture and the weathering of materials, into the simulation of window glass and reflections, and into atmospheric perspective perceived as distance blueing.

CHAPTER 7

More About Equipment – Configurations

In previous chapters we have examined the functions and capabilities of the individual items of equipment. Now we look at some of the ways in which these units are linked together to operate as complete computer configurations.

To do this we shall start again from the user's viewpoint, the workstation. The main components of this were described as the graphics screen, and perhaps an alphanumeric VDU, for monitoring purposes, plus one or more input devices such as a keyboard and data tablet. These and other components may be grouped in various ways to form:

Dumb workstations
Smart workstations
Intelligent workstations.

Dumb workstations
The screens and input devices alone form the workstation and are connected by cables to a host computer. This host contains the processor, memory and mass storage, plus all the CAD software and all the current drawing information. All input data is automatically passed to the host computer for action. This sends a regular supply of data back to the screens so as to keep the user fully informed of the results of the actions, and of the current state of the project. The workstation is therefore limited to input/output functions only.

Intelligent workstations
In addition to the screens and input devices, these have one or more computers plus their associated memory and mass storage built into a complete package. So all the functions of the host computer described above are in fact accommodated within the workstation itself. Thus the whole is a fully self-contained CAD system which normally needs no recourse or connection to any outside element. This means of course that a plotter must be included. Essentially this is a single user, stand-alone CAD system. Examples which we have already met are the Calcomp system and the Cadraw system on the ICL PERQ (refer fig. 7.1).

Smart workstations
These are intermediate between the two extremes described. Microprocessors of some form will be included to give a measure of local graphics processing capability. But the whole will be linked to a host computer. The local processors take some of the load off the host, by undertaking some routine graphics manipulations such as drawing arcs and circles, and generating a variety of line styles and character fonts. So the simpler tasks are

Fig 7.1 'Intelligent' workstation: ICL PERQ (Ove Arup Partnership)

carried out locally but the local processor reverts to the main computer for all tasks beyond its capacity.

The more 'capable' of the smart workstations can operate on a stand-alone basis for much of the time. The current drawing or some section of the relevant drawing information is initially retrieved from the host computer. It is stored in local memory within the workstation. Graphical additions and many alterations can be made to this local copy, and perhaps only at the end of a session is the data returned to update the copy of the information maintained in the host.

PROVISION OF SEVERAL WORKSTATIONS IN A DESIGN OFFICE

When the design office needs more than one workstation to cope with its workload, there are the alternatives of:

1 Multiple workstations (dumb or smart) connected to and sharing one host computer. This is the multiterminal system.
2 Several stand-alone workstations (intelligent), either operating completely independently or linked in some way.

Multiworkstation system

The workstations are normally connected in a star pattern as indicated diagrammatically in fig. 7.2. The host computer is generally a 32-bit supermini processor, examples of which are the DEC VAX, Data General or Prime models (refer to fig. 7.3). These have the power and facilities to manage the sophisticated software. A large information store or database necessary for several design projects can be maintained on the large discs. The several users have access simultaneously to the extensive facilities of the computer's operating system. The ease with which concurrent operations are processed means that expensive peripherals like fast and accurate plotters, printers, hard-copy units and digitisers can be shared effectively between all users.

An advantage of the multiterminal system is that the powerful host processor gives much flexibility to the whole operation. It can respond by constantly directing resources to cope with demands – wherever and whenever they arise.

However the potential problem that can arise with multiworkstation systems must be recognised and avoided. It is that more and more work can be loaded on to the host computer. This can arise from additional workstations attached or merely from a gradual increase in the scale and complexity of projects or of ancillary tasks undertaken. There

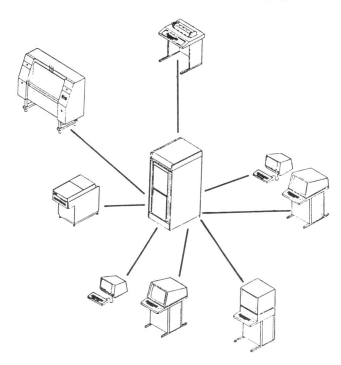

Fig 7.2 Multiworkstation configuration in star pattern

Fig 7.3 Multiterminal computer system: Prime 9950

must come a time when the processor is serving too many masters. It may not completely fail to function, but the problem will manifest itself in lengthening response times perceived by users. The response may become quite unacceptable. Users spend long periods at workstations at drawing input time and their productivity can be adversely affected, sometimes seriously so, if the computer is incapable of keeping up with them.

So it is vital both to install a processor with adequate power and to make some provisions for increasing capacity if it becomes necessary. This is an important topic which will be reserved until later.

Stand-alone workstations
Intelligent workstations have become much more popular in recent times. This is due to the rapid emergence of processors that are physically small and yet have adequate power

for the needs of a single CAD user. The intelligent workstation is ideal for a small organisation which is only ever likely to need one workstation. For larger firms this solution may also appear attractive because it is easy for separate units to be ordered when required and placed where needed in the office. Independence of workstations ensures that performance degradation in the future cannot occur.

However such isolation would mean that two or more people could not work on the same or similar projects at the same time, or at least not without involving difficulties. This is simply because separate databases have to be maintained on each system. Transfer of data from one system to another would have to be done with the aid of magnetic tapes or floppy discs. This is a somewhat slow operation. Where this limitation is not acceptable, a solution might lie in the establishment of direct links or communications between individual systems by networking arrangements.

COMMUNICATIONS BETWEEN CAD SYSTEMS

Local area networks

The traditional way of connecting terminals to a single host computer has been the simple star pattern illustrated in fig. 7.2. This arrangement has much to commend it, including simplicity and cost effectiveness, provided the connections are not excessively long and the terminal locations are fairly fixed. It is not an appropriate method for connecting separate computer processors or intelligent workstations. For these, some form of network is needed. With a growing interest in decentralising computer facilities, the concept of local area networks (LANs) is becoming more important.

A local area network is like a ring main for computer devices. The aim is to be able to plug any computer device, including processors, printers, plotters, microcomputers and various types of terminals, into the network, as shown in fig. 7.4. Each device is linked in by a special transceiver.

There are many different types of local area networks, for example Ethernet, developed by Rank Xerox, and the Cambridge Ring, designed by Cambridge University. Depending on the system adopted, the devices are connected either in 'bus' formation or to a cable forming a complete ring. In principle, the transceivers create 'packets' of data and each packet contains a coded source and destination address. The cable itself can be just a twisted pair of wires, or a coaxial cable might be required. When one device needs to send data, its transceiver listens to see if the network is idle, before projecting a data packet into it. The transceiver serving the destination device will accept the packet out of the network and deliver it. It will ignore all other packets.

In theory such networks are a means of connecting disparate equipment together and a way of shifting pieces of data around an organisation. One application is the integration of several single user CAD systems in such a way that a single disc could function as the primary drawing store. A single plotter could provide plotting facilities for the whole network. For such a task a simple 'baseband' network would be appropriate. At the other extreme, sophisticated 'broadband' network systems can deal with a broader number of channels capable of carrying more than one kind of data at once, such as digital data and speech communications.

An advantage with networking is that it is possible to add in extra workstations or other devices to the network without too much effort. In practice, the pitfalls can be that different proprietary networks vary in capabilities and cost. The range of devices that can be connected still depends on interfaces, and standards in this area are not completely settled.

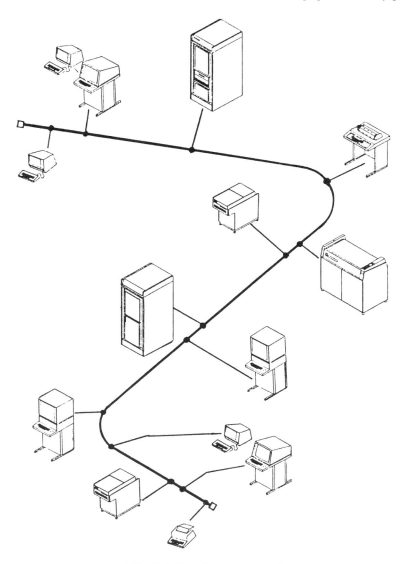

Fig 7.4 Local area network

The local area network is designed to cope with the needs of an organisation at a single site. The maximum length of the Ethernet system for instance is 2.5 km. It will not provide the complete answer for an organisation that has got its drawing office facilities dispersed at greater distances.

Multiple sites

Computer graphics involve the movement of large volumes of data. In principle it is preferable to confine these data transfers to hard wires whenever possible. Telecommunications techniques are improving rapidly, but progress is not on a par with the pace of computer processor development. So where there are entirely separate drawing offices it is best, at least initially, to confine all the CAD operation to one of the sites. If this is not convenient then the choice must lie between:

1 A separate system in each office
2 A separate system in each office but with telecommunication links between processors

3 One central computer with workstations at remote offices linked by telecommunications.

SEPARATE SYSTEMS — WITHOUT LINKS
Entirely separate systems are the answer if the work of each office involves different projects, different disciplines or is otherwise more or less independent. Of course this solution presupposes that there is sufficient work to justify a system in each place. It can be argued that it is easier to manage a single large computer than two or more small ones, but the modern mini is becoming very easy to manage in any case. Fairly infrequent transfers of data could be accommodated with magnetic tapes, floppy discs or cartridge disc units.

LINKING SEPARATE COMPUTER SYSTEMS
Separate systems can sometimes be linked either by direct high capacity cables or through telecommunications channels. The efficiency depends on the data transfer rate through the links that is needed and on the effectiveness of the communications software.

Where the connected computers are supplied by the same manufacturer, though not necessarily being all the same model, then quite sophisticated operations can be possible. For example a user connected to any one processor can decide where his processing is to be done and can specify the site at which his database resides. Several of the minicomputer manufacturers can provide the necessary hardware and software; for example, PRIMENET can link all current models of Prime processors together.

When dissimilar computers are involved, only fairly basic transfers of data files from one system to another, or simple interactive communications, might be possible. Even this depends on the availability of hardware interfaces and software packages known as emulators. In time, however, there will be efficient and cost effective wide area networks (WANs) for this purpose. These may even use satellite communications to link separate local area networks together.

REMOTE WORKSTATIONS
The supplier of a system can advise on the maximum distance at which hard-wired workstations can be located from the computer. Sometimes this extends to 2000 metres or more, assuming direct cable routes are feasible. It might be only 50 metres, however, so this point needs careful checking. It is increasingly common for facilities to be required well beyond such limitations.

Some types of workstation can be remotely connected to a processor using a telecommunications channel with a modem at each end. A modem is an item of equipment which must be interposed between a computer device and a telephone line. Its function is to convert the signals from the device into a form suitable for passing along the telephone line, and the reverse process. The possibility of connecting a workstation in this way needs to be checked out with the supplier. For CAD work, such remote working requires high data transfer rates, higher than are possible with the dial-up facilities used for many conventional computer terminals. So either a leased telephone line or the public packet switching network must be used. The use of leased lines usually involves an installation fee and an annual rental which depends on the length of the circuit. Packet switching costs are independent of distance, but relate to the volume of data actually transmitted. A leased line is best for intensive use over relatively short distances. If the operation is to be rather intermittent, then packet switching might be cheaper.

Remote working often needs smart workstations. Also the software used must create compact data structures for transfer. As already described, some systems transmit a part of the drawing database, and store this in the workstation where it can be edited and added to. Only at the end of a session is it finally transmitted back to the distant host computer.

If more than one device is required to operate simultaneously at a remote site, then a separate telecommunication channel must be used for each. Alternatively it is possible to install a multiplexer device at each end of a single channel. Multiplexers pack the data streams from the separate devices for sending down the single line and unpack the incoming signals. Careful consideration needs to be given to the data transfer rates of the individual devices, and to the capacity of the channel. Remote plotting often presents problems if anything more than simple drawings are involved.

UPGRADING EQUIPMENT

Everyone is well aware of the rapid pace of development of computer equipment. Many are also acutely aware that existing equipment can be rendered obsolescent by newer products and methods long before they are physically worn out. This frightens many off investing in the first place. Some people fear that their drawing data built up over a period and held in computer stores will in time be rendered useless by such obsolescence. For owners of CAD systems, there is also the likelihood that with increasing confidence, greater awareness of possibilities of CAD, or merely with an unforeseen rising workload, their system will have to be made bigger. All these matters make it necessary to consider carefully the subject of upgrading systems.

The computer industry is slowly facing and coming to terms with this problem. If proper attention is given to the matter at the time of system selection, it can be minimised – and it must.

The essential fact to be grasped is that a computer is not a single 'black box' which is purchased, used for a few years, and finally discarded and replaced with a better one. It is more useful to think of a computer as a configuration of several interconnected black boxes, each of which has a function. At some time in the future, the system might be upgraded by:

Upgrading individual black boxes by modification or adding in new components; or
Adding more black boxes; or
Replacing individual black boxes by better ones.

This can be illustrated by reference to the central processor of a multiterminal system. Processing capacity might be stepped up to keep ahead of demand by:

Adding more memory boards, effectively permitting the existing CPU to work faster; or

Adding another processor. This could be put in to form the nucleus of a completely separate system, or it could be connected in some way into the existing system; or

Replacing the CPU by a similar but more powerful model from the manufacturer's range.

This of course presupposes that the particular processor selected can be upgraded in these ways. Similarly it might be feasible to increase disc capacity, add a magnetic tape drive or upgrade the plotter, or to add workstations or improve existing ones say by fitting data tablets. So it is easily possible to envisage the situation where the total hardware system never actually becomes obsolete. Instead, some items are added from time to time and others are discarded.

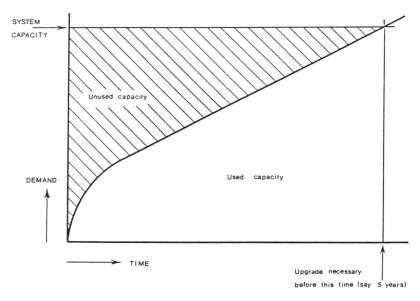

Fig 7.5 Upgrade of configuration in single jump

It might be felt that the system must be planned with enough inbuilt hardware capacity to cater for a considerable period, say five years. This option is illustrated by fig. 7.5. The alternative is to install a smaller system and to be prepared to upgrade more frequently, as indicated in fig. 7.6.

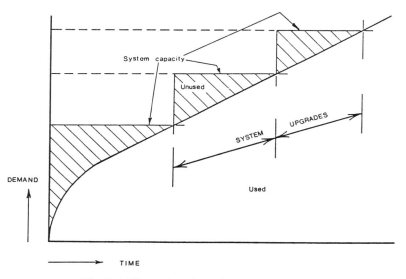

Fig 7.6 Upgrade of configuration in stages

The first option has some merit in that economies of scale are available because a larger capacity system is being sought. Also it is a fact that most organisations underestimate their computer requirements in the first place. Nevertheless, in the early days, much capacity could remain idle or underused, and this is unnecessarily expensive. Obsolescence always looms and in the uncertain future there is never much of a guarantee anyway that any installation will always have adequate capacity.

So it is often better to deliberately proceed in a step-by-step manner. It means installing an initial system that is smaller but is easily upgradable in various ways. Then ideally we

Fig 7.7 Prime 2250 minicomputer system

need to keep just ahead of demand and to be prepared to invest when necessary. The merits of this course are:

1 It may well be the cheaper solution overall when the continually reducing hardware costs are taken into account. Part of the cash flow is deferred and so could be discounted to allow for this fact.
2 It is a more flexible approach. It is easier to take advantage of future hardware developments. For example a workstation added later on might include a colour screen.

It is possible to distinguish between upgrades in scale, and upgrades in facilities. Scale upgrades are to provide for increased, perhaps unforeseen, demand. These are dealt with by increased processor power, increased disc capacity, more workstations and so on. Upgrades in facilities, in terms of hardware, are more difficult to predict and to provide for. Adding colour capacity in workstations, remote terminals, or screens with more advanced hardware pan and zoom facilities, are some examples.

A CAD system comprising a number of intelligent workstations, possibly connected into a LAN, is simple to upgrade. Basically, when more capacity is needed the latest model of workstation available is purchased and added to the net. Even existing workstations can be modified in some circumstances. For example it might become feasible to change the display tube for one with a higher resolution, or one with colour.

HOUSING THE EQUIPMENT – ENVIRONMENTAL FACTORS

Mainframe computers used to be extremely demanding in this respect. They were physically large and the temperature, humidity and cleanliness of the surroundings all had to be closely controlled.

Fortunately the modern minicomputer is much more robust. Typically the processor will tolerate an operating environment of 5–50°C and from 10–95% relative humidity. However the large exchangeable disc drives are a little more demanding, with a temperature range of perhaps 15–32°C, a humidity of 20–80% and a dust-free room being necessary. The environmental requirements need to be checked most carefully before planning computer accommodation.

Although these limits appear wide, in practice a minicomputer and main peripherals might produce say 4 kW of heat. So some air conditioning will be necessary if the system is housed in a small room. A reasonably powerful system can be accommodated in a space of about 15 m², but the exact layout of items needs to be agreed with the supplier. In particular he will want some free space around cabinets for maintenance access.

A new range of physically small but high performance 32-bit superminis is appearing, typified by the Prime 2250 (fig. 7.7). This processor has adequate capacity to operate three or more CAD workstations. However it is compact, has a smaller heat and noise output, and perhaps no special computer room needs to be provided. It might instead be accommodated within the normal office surroundings. This is an important consideration since the provision of a computer room would otherwise be a significant added expense.

Intelligent, stand-alone workstations are similarly undemanding as regards their environment.

CHAPTER 8
Is there a Need for CAD?

When an office first begins to appreciate that it may need a CAD system, positive action in the shape of some form of feasibility study must be carried out. This chapter deals with the setting up, the aims, and some of the early activities of such a study. Before becoming too deeply immersed in time consuming investigations of individual systems, it is important to determine just how serious is the commitment of the organisation. So we will enumerate and discuss some of the potential benefits of CAD.

THE AWAKENING TO A NEED FOR CAD

Sometimes there are people in the organisation who have been watching the progress of CAD for a long time. They have tried to keep themselves informed and have been waiting patiently for the technique to become more practical and economic.

In other cases, somebody becomes enthusiastic after a visit to an exhibition or conference, or after seeing a demonstration or reading a magazine article. Sometimes the spur to action is a growing feeling that, without CAD, the organisation is falling behind others in the technology race. In a highly competitive situation this cannot be permitted to endure for long. Others see it in a more positive light, as something which will give them a competitive edge in the marketing of their design services. In the minds of many people, computers are still associated with efficient and progressive managements. Although this is not universally true, it is completely justified in the majority of cases.

The trigger might be the arrival of a single large project, or just a growing workload which increases the general confidence level or improves the financial climate of the organisation. Perhaps the increasing workload threatens to overload the existing staff. Then the adoption of a CAD system is seen as a way of preventing an increase in staff numbers and/or the need to move to bigger offices. Just occasionally one hears of an organisation with the choice of spending its money on a CAD system, or of giving it away in tax.

These are some of the things that can kindle an interest in a CAD system.

The use of computers for business and technical applications may already be well established within the firm. Such applications are increasingly diverse. They might include accounting, word processing, data collection, storage and retrieval of information, project management, as well as calculations associated with design and analysis. There might be a computer or data processing department with a DP manager or an equivalent who coordinates all computing work within the company. In many places, the business use of computers has taken priority. It is then quite common for drawing office staff and computer specialists to feel rather distant from one another with little real understanding of the others' role.

The interest in CAD might emerge in either the drawing office or the computer department. In practice it can be difficult for this early enthusiasm to progress beyond the pipe-dream stage because of the remoteness of the parties that would be most deeply involved. In professional firms it is often the partners or directors who initiate action, and indeed in most places nothing much can or indeed should happen until top management has become interested.

This need for a commitment at high level is vital. It must be recognised that long before an order for a CAD system can be placed, an exhaustive study will have to be undertaken. This cannot be dodged. Whatever potential benefits might be available, the implications of choosing an inappropriate system or of applying one in the wrong circumstances can be very damaging. The selection process is itself a very complex affair. Anyone undertaking a study will need much free time. He will have to grapple with new concepts, cope with computer jargon and absorb facts and opinions about items of hardware, software, and costs. He must make a realistic assessment of the benefits and potential problems. Above all it is an exercise in management planning because the work pattern of many individuals will be radically changed. This may sound offputting, but the benefits of CAD can be large. They will be discussed later on.

When an organisation seriously contemplates using computers for the first time, most thought is often devoted to the hardware. This may result from pressure exerted by hardware salesmen or merely from a general fascination with the amazing hardware developments of recent times. Frequently attention is focused on the potential of the physical equipment rather than on analysing the real requirements of the office or available programs. Too often, equipment and programs are selected for a limited application. Later, when skills and knowledge expand, the installed hardware/software combination is found to be unsuitable or to have too limited a capacity for the broadening needs and interests of the organisation.

So it is sensible to try to create some overall strategy and to determine priorities for the whole organisation. When the main aims and the software possibilities have been identified, the hardware choice will often have been narrowed considerably, and solutions will become more obvious. In this way, expensive mistakes by novice organisations are likely to be avoided.

So who must be the 'standard bearer' for CAD? If there is a data processing manager, he would face difficulties. Apart from a remoteness from drawing office practice and procedures, much of the hardware is of a specialist nature. He is unlikely to have an up-to-date awareness of the specialist CAD market. The drawing office people would be in a superior position to determine their needs and aims, and to judge the practical capabilities of any system on offer. However they would be in grave danger of becoming thoroughly confused by the plethora of hardware and software available. Top management might be better able to take a more balanced view, but could find the demands on their time daunting.

An independent consultant, provided he has suitable experience and knowledge, may be able to contribute much in this situation. However an experience of technical computing alone is completely inadequate for the reasons already enumerated. A consultant having limited practical experience or experience of only one system can be a menace. So the consultant must have prior experience of the discipline of the application, of several CAD systems and of their introduction in other places. Inevitably, however, he would lack the detailed knowledge of the aims, aspirations and operation of the organisation and of the personalities involved. Thus a suitably experienced external consultant could contribute much, but he could not do the work unaided.

So it seems likely that the standard bearer for CAD cannot be a single individual but must be a small team. The members ought to include someone from top management because of the importance of the subject to the organisation. Clearly it ought to include a drawing office representative, a computer person perhaps, and an external consultant with proven CAD experience. The task of the team is to carry out a feasibility study.

AIMS OF FEASIBILITY STUDY

These should be as follows:

To seek more background information on CAD
To identify applications which might benefit from the use of CAD methods
To consider the potential benefits to the organisation
To determine the main options available
To draw up a list of those factors which will govern the choice of system – the selection criteria.

Assuming that the team remains committed to the concept, it ought now to seek approval to progress to the next phase of its work. This next phase tends to be rather time consuming:

To draw up a list of possible suppliers
To study individual systems and arrive at a conclusion as to which would be the best choice for the organisation.

Assuming all necessary approvals to proceed are then forthcoming:

To make arrangements for all the financial and contractual matters involved in the placing of an order with the chosen supplier
To plan for the introduction and management of the system.

COMMENTS ON STUDY PROCEDURE

It would be foolish to suggest that all the tasks listed above can always be undertaken as a step-by-step procedure in the manner and precise order given. It is much more likely to be an iterative process. So there may in practice be a gradual increase in CAD knowledge, a growing appreciation of the potential applications and benefits, and a developing awareness of the systems on the market. If a list of selection criteria can be drafted early on, then it is likely to be continually modified and improved until a contract with a supplier is actually signed. It is also only realistic to note that at present most organisations jump straight in and the bulk of their detailed knowledge of CAD comes directly from visits, demonstrations and discussions with potential suppliers.

In small firms, the assessment may well be carried out mainly by one person, and this is necessary because resources are severely limited. But then lines of communication are short and he is likely to be in constant dialogue with his colleagues.

Indeed it has to be said that circumstances vary so widely that only a rough guide can be given here, to be interpreted in the individual situation. Nevertheless the procedure along the above lines is recommended strongly in the belief that:

1 A purchasing organisation should not gain the bulk of its knowledge from the suppliers. Such action usually puts the customer at a commercial disadvantage.

2 Potential CAD applications need to be studied early on, otherwise much time can be wasted on assessing systems and methods that are not in fact relevant.

3 Identification of the potential benefits should come early on. CAD systems are costly and even the feasibility study itself is expensive. The benefits may be even larger, but it is important to gain support, and to continue receiving support from all quarters. Management needs to receive assurances that it is all worth while, and even the team needs these if it is to remain purposeful. On the other hand, if significant benefits to match the costs and disruptions cannot be found, or the money will not be forthcoming for some external reason, then the feasibility study ought to be aborted before much time is spent in assessing individual products.

4 It is better to be clear about the options available and to list some criteria before setting out to assess lots of systems. This again saves much time. Also the criteria ought to be set out without too much help, well intentioned or otherwise, from individual suppliers. It is only reasonable that they will try to guide the customer towards features of the supplier's choice. In short, they are biased.

Of necessity, this study must be carried out over a period of time. Naturally it needs to be a part time activity for the participants. It would be unreasonable to assume that it can be done in a few weeks. Some firms take a very long time, and indeed a period of two years or more is not too uncommon. But if the procedure is allowed to be too drawn out, the technology and the market will be changing before the very eyes of the team!

In this chapter we will discuss the acquisition of CAD knowledge, identification of applications and the potential benefits of CAD. The next chapter will cover the options available. Chapter 10 deals with the selection criteria and investigation of available turnkey systems.

ACQUIRING KNOWLEDGE OF CAD MARKET

Initially there may be a lack of understanding of CAD. There is going to be a strong temptation to just seek appointments with CAD suppliers merely to improve the general knowledge in this new subject. This is rather unfair on these companies, and possibly unwise for the reasons already stated. Suppliers have in the past found themselves loaded with most of the burden of educating the marketplace. But CAD companies are now more adept at spotting and attending to the serious prospect who has clearly done his homework already.

Unfortunately it is far from easy to obtain up-to-date knowledge in this field. Educational establishments including universities are finding it difficult to provide appropriate training. This is due to the expense involved in acquiring up-to-date equipment of adequate power and relevant software. Also their teaching staffs have understandable difficulties in acquiring practical experience. So it may be necessary to rely more on technical literature and conferences, and on exhibitions where potential suppliers are more easily approached.

Companies that have already embarked on CAD and are willing to share some of their experience are another valuable source of knowledge. Again these are best identified from friends and from the grapevine rather than contacting those firms recommended by suppliers. Curiously, in such a competitive world, firms often seem quite willing to share some of their experiences. Perhaps in some way they are repaying to others a debt incurred when they too needed such assistance. It is of course unreasonable to expect such firms to be critical of the system which they have, to admit to any errors on their part, or to have much knowledge of other systems or their relative merits.

It must be clearly understood here that no system can be the optimum for all situations. Even if two organisations were almost identical in all their needs – a highly improbable situation – the range of systems on offer in the marketplace changes rapidly in even a short time. So the temptation to merely copy unquestioningly what has been done elsewhere must be resisted at all costs.

In fact it cannot be stressed too strongly that the team must do its homework carefully and conscientiously. The risks are great. A firm that makes a superficial examination of its needs and then orders an unsuitable or inadequate system has made a serious error. Not only would much money have been spent directly on unsuitable equipment and software, but much staff time will be expended in training and in creating many drawings before the facts become fully known.

Obviously the necessary knowledge and skills are very unlikely to exist in a firm that does not already employ the relevant techniques and systems. In practice an external consultant can be helpful in these circumstances, provided he has the qualities previously mentioned. Indeed industrial and professional management require an enormous amount of such support from external consultants if they are to come to grips with such rapidly advancing technologies.

POTENTIAL APPLICATIONS AND A LOOK AT THE EXISTING ARRANGEMENTS

It is impossible here to lay down specific guidelines on how to evaluate the potential applications for CAD in any organisation. Broadly, however the existing pattern of design work needs to be examined to determine the true nature and approximate quantities of drawings that are now produced or expected in the future. There may be drawings done by different disciplines. Certainly different types of drawings will be appearing at different stages in projects. First there are the early creative drawings or sketch designs. Later the general arrangements at various scales are produced, and later still come the detail drawings and record drawings of various types.

A study of drawings will indicate the degree of repetition and the potential cost savings and other benefits which might be obtained from CAD. Obviously repeated use of standard components, symbols and standard details would stand out like a beacon. However work of this nature is not particularly widespread and so cannot always be expected. But it is surprising how a deeper examination of the workload and a greater understanding of the potential of CAD reveals similar, but maybe not identical components and details recurring many times. Above all there may well be a great deal of general arrangement material repeated at different scales for different purposes by different disciplines at different times in a project. Indeed such an examination may well reveal an abundance of repetitive work.

However repetition is just one item to be considered. The pattern of information flow is important. It is relevant to enquire into where exactly the information that ends up on drawings is coming from, where the drawings are being created and how the information flows between these points. The backgrounds, capabilities, personalities and availability of people concerned in the process need looking at. Where are the shortages, the bottlenecks, the inefficiencies, the problems, both now and in the future?

A decision will have to be taken on which of the following is to be aimed for:

1 Complete conversion to CAD methods of the whole of the organisation's draughting workload in one step.
2 Partial conversion to CAD, i.e. installing computer capacity for a part of the

workload and leaving the rest to be attended to later, perhaps when more experience of CAD has been gained.

3 Installation of a CAD system to provide additional capacity for an increasing workload.

With a small drawing office, it might well be easier to convert to CAD methods as rapidly and completely as possible. Large offices may be too vulnerable during such a traumatic experience. They may find it better to phase the change over several years. It is important to bear in mind that a CAD system must be kept busy if it is to benefit the purchaser. Idle equipment, like idle people, costs money.

Estimates must be made of the number of drawings that the CAD system will be required to cope with. The quantity must be related to the size and degree of complexity or density of typical drawings. Some idea will be needed of the number of distinct projects to be undertaken in parallel. Also a rough idea is required of the numbers of drawings that will need to be stored simultaneously in a rapidly accessible form. The rate of production of hard-copy drawings and any related schedules must be thought about as well. All this, as well as the numbers of draughtsmen available for training in CAD methods, will be needed later on. The potential suppliers can use this to estimate the size and composition of the computer system required. Only then can the all-important system costs be evaluated.

In this process the quantity of drawings normally created for internal communications, within the confines of the design team, needs to be evaluated. These require resources like other drawings. They perform a valuable function but they do not actually end up among the tally of finished project drawings. Obviously they must not be ignored in the workload estimates.

POTENTIAL BENEFITS

One aim of the feasibility study is to identify potential benefits. A convincing case will have to be built up to prove that these will outweigh the direct and indirect costs of a system, plus any drawbacks that might be expected.

It is a fact that most of the benefits are of an intangible nature and cannot be quantified easily. However, just because they are intangible, they ought not be neglected or considered as unimportant. Some of the more obvious ones are now discussed. Clearly the advantages gained depend much on the organisation itself, on the system used, and on the manner of its use. Several of the items mentioned are interrelated.

Reduced lead times Reduced project costs	By reducing the time taken for initial design concept through to the finished construction drawings, it should be possible to go out to tender earlier and with more complete design information available. This ought to have a beneficial effect on tender values and this may be large compared with the design costs.
Same information used throughout	The information created for scheme design is not discarded. It could be worked up by adding more and more detail, and this forms the basis of construction drawings, and later still of construction record drawings.
Build-up of experience Standard details	Components and details created for one project can be saved in libraries and used in future projects. In normal work, standard details are

usually difficult to apply because circumstances on the new job often call for slight modifications. With CAD it is easy to store details. When retrieved later, they can be used unchanged, but it is very easy to adapt them slightly as and when necessary to suit the new circumstances. They do not need to be redrawn completely.

Able to coordinate design documentation more easily	Systems that can be used for scheduling, and which permit coordination of plans, elevations, and sections are better in this respect.
Able to coordinate different disciplines more easily	Designers of different disciplines are more likely to be aware of the current intentions of the others. Their information is more up to date.
Dimensional reliability and precision improved	Dimensions throughout are not constantly being recalculated over and over again by different people for different purposes. The basic project geometry is held in the data model and most dimensions are calculated automatically by the CAD system itself.
Fewer gross errors	Each designer is using the same data model and there is less chance of erroneously placed items. Clashing of components is more likely to show up.
Rapid modifications Improved quality of design Increased speed of response to changes	Major modifications can be easily made to a whole series of drawings, e.g. moving a grid line and all elements related to it. This can lead to improved designs and better projects because designers are less concerned about making major changes in the drawings. Without CAD they are inhibited because of the large investment of time that would be needed.
Improved quality of drawings	Drawing quality should be more consistent and of a generally higher standard. It is easier to impose a house standard.
Easier to communicate with clients	With some systems 3-D views can be created quickly from a variety of viewpoints. Then the objectives and intentions of the designer can be more easily appreciated and understood by clients and lay people.
Able to create new drawings easily	This can be done by scaling and bringing together layers in various combinations, and by merging or breaking up details.
Can freeze design and plot drawings later	The design information can be frozen and then all the project drawings can be plotted on paper almost at the last moment, e.g. just before going out to tender.

Greater job satisfaction

The CAD users can spend less time on routine tasks such as copying background information at different scales on new drawings, copying details, and producing schedules laboriously by hand. They can therefore spend more time on the execution of creative design.

INCREASED DRAWING PRODUCTIVITY

This item has been left to the last. Most people actively involved with CAD believe fairly strongly that drawing productivity is increased substantially. Nearly always, however, this is their subjective judgement, because few can prove it by pointing to reduced numbers of people.

This is not too surprising because few organisations have been using CAD for long. Even fewer have the time to undertake controlled tests by doing the same design work by CAD and then by traditional methods so as to compare them.

If an item or detail occurred only once on the drawings, there would be little, if any, gain. It may take just as long to draw a one-off item by CAD as it would take by hand – perhaps longer. But projects that superficially appear to contain little repetition, in fact may do so, as a closer examination often shows.

Many people claim that a productivity factor of about 3 is usually attained over a long period. However it is unwise to generalise about productivity factors. They can be expected to vary widely. They depend on the project – its size, the disciplines involved, the degree of repetition and the complexity. They depend on the system, and on the operators' skill and experience. They also vary, depending on the amount of background information already maintained by the office in computer held libraries and in data models for other projects. So for highly repetitive work the productivity factor might be 10:1 or more, in certain other cases it might be 1:1 or worse.

The next problem is that different people sometimes mean different things when they quote such figures. Suppliers are particularly susceptible to this. To be consistent, a productivity factor must relate to the increased turnout of drawing work that an operator can produce compared with hand methods *during the time when he is actually engaged in drawing work.*

COST/BENEFIT ANALYSIS

It is perhaps understandable that few organisations attempt a cost/benefit study, claiming that such a thing is impossible. Many of those that have undertaken one are not too confident about its accuracy. But it is a rather unsatisfactory state of affairs that such a large investment is nearly always made on purely subjective judgement of the potential benefits.

Yet for many professional firms, the acquisition of a CAD system is the most expensive capital investment that they are likely to make. Unlike an industrial firm whose management is more accustomed to investing in plant and factories, the professional firm may only be used to investing in the recurring costs of staff salaries and rents. To them the sums involved seem huge, even though the cost of a two-workstation system when spread over five years might be no more than the cost of one designer and his overheads.

A rudimentary cost/benefit study might be done on the following lines: Consider a design office with a number of designers/draughtsmen who each work 7.5 hours per day. Assume that at present they work on average one-third of their time at the drawing board, and the rest at other duties such as information gathering, meetings and so on. Assume that with overheads, each costs 20 000 CU per year to employ (where CU stands for currency unit: the individual reader can substitute reasonable figures in his own currency).

Consider what happens in the future if a CAD system is introduced and drawing productivity increases on average by a factor of 3:

Now: Each person spends 33% of the time on drawing.
        Each person spends 67% of the time on other duties.
Future: He spends 11% of the time doing the same drawings by CAD.
        He spends 67% on other duties, as before.

So he will achieve the same result in 78% of the time. In a given period, he will achieve 22/78 = 28% more. In one year, the saving will be 20 000 × 0.28 = 5600 CU. Each person will need on average 11/78 = 14% of their time at a workstation. This is 0.14 × 7.5 = 1.05 hours per day.

Assume that each workstation will be available for use during a 10 hour day, and flexible working hours will be in operation.

Each workstation will cope with the work of 10/1.05 = 9.5 persons. Reduce this to 8 persons to make allowance for late starts, some idle time at changeovers, maintenance etc.

We conclude that each workstation could save 5600 × 8 = 44 800 CU annually. If all the costs involved in providing each workstation will be less than this figure, then the organisation will benefit.

Each reader could substitute his own figures and assumptions, and arrive at his own conclusion.

The main items that contribute to costs are:

1 Capital cost of system – equipment and software.
2 Costs of feasibility study and administration involved in contract for supply.
3 System maintenance costs – equipment and software.
4 Cost of providing any additional floor space needed for computer and workstations, including capital costs of additional services such as air conditioning, special electricity supply, etc. Recurring items such as rent, rates, lighting, heating, etc.
5 Cost of insurance of equipment.
6 Cost of power supply for equipment.
7 Cost of consumables, such as plotting paper, magnetic tapes.
8 System staffing and management costs.

Total system costs are simply divided by the number of workstations to arrive at a cost for each. It is important to include the cost of the plotter in the total system costs, so that this is apportioned to each workstation.

Clearly the bulk of the costs are fixed items. It follows that the longer the hours worked in the day and the more intensively the system is operated, the more cost effective it is likely to be.

Accurate costs can only be defined when the system is chosen and a computer configuration suitable for the firm is identified. Before that time estimates have to be used. Eventually when the costs are known accurately, the one item that remains in some doubt is the productivity factor. It might be instructive to work the calculation backwards, and determine the productivity factor that must be achieved to break even.

It could be easier to come to a conclusion in the matter if it could be reduced to something along the lines:

> We are aware of a number of additional benefits that are important to us, but they are intangible. However, if this system can give us an average productivity factor of 2.4 (say) or more, then even neglecting all the intangibles it is worth while.

Rapid obsolescence of equipment is a problem that has been mentioned already. This is sometimes made the excuse for not investing at all. Alternatively it encourages firms to put off investment until something even better or cheaper becomes available. Yet if an investment appears to give an adequate return based on a reasonably short product life of say four to five years, then it seems unwise to deny oneself of the immediate benefits.

CHAPTER 9
The Options

For an organisation setting out to acquire or gain access to a CAD system, the options are:

1 Deal with a computer bureaux
2 Acquire a turnkey system
3 Acquire software for existing computer
4 Acquire software and equipment from separate sources
5 Write or commission writing of software.

COMPUTER BUREAUX

These companies operate computer machinery and offer their customers access to this. Users can physically go to the computer to operate terminals, but increasingly access is from remote terminals linked by telephone line or other means.

Bureaux tend to specialise in one application area and this is reflected in the type of computer operated, in the software available, and in the expertise of the support staff. Comparatively few bureaux yet specialise in CAD but this may change.

Under the heading of computer bureaux, mention can be made of those companies that have installed CAD systems, then by design or accident have found themselves with surplus capacity which they are offering to others. Useful and perhaps cost effective arrangements might be established with such firms. However the surplus capacity can evaporate quickly and the potential user with more than a short term requirement would need to enquire into how continuity of service will be maintained.

Some firms do not concentrate on merely offering their equipment, software and support, but also offer the services of experienced workstation operators or consultancy services.

There are several advantages of bureaux:

1 There is no capital or other resources tied up in equipment and software, its accommodation, management and support. Instead, access is possible when desired to expensive equipment, software and maybe to experienced staff.
2 There is a short lead time before the facility can be used.
3 Since minimum charges are small or non-existent, it can be appropriate for small scale work, for feasibility studies or other work before a main job has been secured.
4 It is a source of additional capacity when the in-house CAD facility is temporarily overloaded or otherwise when time is of the essence.

5 It is possible to gain some experience with CAD and indeed to evaluate the CAD system in use with no obligations. At the same time, drawings can be produced for a project.

These must be weighed against some disadvantages of using computer bureaux for CAD work, such as:

1 Charges for the service are normally based on resources actually used by the customer and they can be at high rates. Total costs are difficult to predict, and no concessions are likely for abortive work.
2 The equipment is remote in every sense unless workstations can be sited in the customer's own offices and linked to the bureau. Workstations linked by telephone may not operate at a high enough data transfer rate to permit reasonable response times and efficient working. Dial-up facilities may well be too slow for most CAD work and call charges may mount up particularly if the bureau is located beyond the local call charge area. Higher speeds are possible with leased telephone lines but there are costs of hiring lines, modems and perhaps multiplexers.
3 The CAD software offered may not be appropriate for the type of work in hand, and the operating or support staff at the bureau may not be familiar with the work discipline.

In some circumstances it might not be cost effective to use a computer bureau for long term or 'baseload' CAD applications. But it is clear that there will be a continuing role for them to play in the future.

The important parameters in selecting a bureau are:

1 The suitability of the CAD software for the task in hand
2 The capabilities, personalities and availability of support staff
3 The speed of response obtainable at the workstation
4 Costs.

TURNKEY SYSTEMS

When a firm contracts to supply a major piece of software, plus a complete hardware configuration to run it on, then the hardware/software combination is known as a turnkey system.

Usually a turnkey firm builds up its expertise over a long period of time. This expertise is in the form of application software that runs on a suitable range of computers. So with a turnkey system, the customer should be buying a kit of equipment and programs which demonstratively can work in unison without interfacing or other undefined problems. Indeed the whole may well have been carefully tuned to operate very effectively together. The customer needs no programming staff, and the whole facility can be operated virtually on the day on which the hardware is delivered. Commissioning of the system, training of the customer's staff, and maintenance of hardware and software, are all items which are covered in a contract with the one supplier. The majority of CAD systems in use in the construction industry have been installed under this type of contract.

There are disadvantages. The whole system will have been designed expressly to appeal to the maximum number of potential customers. It is therefore not tailored to the specific needs of an individual organisation. So it cannot cater for all specialist requirements. Therefore the turnkey system is always something of a compromise.

It never should be overlooked that the customer is in effect tying himself to, and making himself to some extent dependent on, the supplier in a long term arrangement. All programs need to be maintained and CAD programs are more complex than most. Extending into the future, the supplier must remain fully committed and fully capable of giving the necessary support and maintenance. After a turnkey contract is signed, the customer cannot lightly change course and switch to a better system if the first is subsequently found to be unsuitable. Quite apart from the sizeable initial direct investment with the supplier, there is the growing investment in terms of trained staff, and the growing database of drawings held in digital form. This will not be compatible with any alternative system. Hence the importance of choosing correctly first time.

The customer will probably have to rely entirely on the supplier for improvements or enhancements to the system in future years, and perhaps also for the supply of more specialised but related software. For example after installing a general-purpose draughting system, a customer might well develop a need for a reinforced concrete detailing capability, for scheduling or costing ability, or for an interface with a third party environmental design program. Will the original turnkey supplier have the capability or interest in fulfilling this need? A tie with a single turnkey supplier is no disadvantage if the firm is thrusting, enthusiastic, committed to the marketplace and constantly developing useful new ideas and techniques. But the opposite is true if the firm stagnates.

It may now be appreciated that there can be a large difference between a turnkey firm that has developed the software itself, and a supplier that is merely acting as an agent for the software authors.

ACQUIRING SOFTWARE FOR EXISTING COMPUTERS

If there are one or more existing computers within the organisation, then we need to assess their suitability for CAD work.

Sometimes even a cursory look at the existing facilities may discourage the idea of mounting CAD applications on them. But it would be unwise to give up without some assessment. It is wise therefore to enquire into the purpose, function, existing workload, capacity and potential of the existing set-up.

First of all, there may be little or no spare capacity. CAD could be expected to impose a substantial new burden on the processor and storage capacity. This fact alone need not be a complete deterrent, because it may well be possible to upgrade the equipment. We need to be realistic, however, for in practice the upgrade necessary may be to a more powerful processor or at least for more memory, plus more mass storage, plus workstations and plotter – for these last elements probably do not yet exist within the organisation. It almost amounts to a whole new hardware configuration.

If this seems daunting, we should still not reject the option yet. For whether a major upgrade is needed or even a entirely new computer configuration, there are arguments for staying with just one computer manufacturer if possible. The arguments relate to such matters as staff familiarity with the operation of the equipment and the disadvantages inherent in dealing with too many suppliers. Needless to say, such arguments must not override all others completely.

If use of an existing computer remains an option, then a search must be made to see if there are CAD software packages on the market that will operate on the equipment. The hardware supplier will be a good source of information. If there is none to be found, then this is indeed a block on further progress along these particular lines. Even so, it might still be possible to persuade a CAD software firm to modify its programs to suit the computer. This is somewhat unlikely because in practice software firms do not like to dissipate their technical expertise too widely, and this is understandable. After all, they would have to maintain the software on this equipment, and this would be a long term commitment which probably would not be attractive to them. In any case, the lack of a CAD package is itself a strong indication that maybe the hardware is not very suitable for interactive graphics work.

On the other hand, if a CAD software package is identified, this remains one option only. The selection of second best software for such an important application just because it fits the existing computer would be very unwise. Software selection should dominate, and the best available CAD software should be obtained even if it involves the installation of a new computer.

SOFTWARE AND EQUIPMENT FROM SEPARATE SOURCES

This is the main alternative to a turnkey system.

A complete hardware configuration might be obtainable from a computer manufacturer or other single source. This, however, is not always possible in view of the wide range of devices needed for a typical CAD system. No single firm makes the whole range of processors, discs, plotters, graphics screens and so on. So in practice it often means that equipment must come from more than one source, perhaps several. It follows that responsibility for ensuring that all items are correctly interfaced and operate in harmony rests with the purchaser. This is not a task to undertake lightly and is not for beginners. It might be done if the organisation already has competent and experienced computer personnel or with the help of an external consultant.

This is an option which may be attractive to the large organisation which does not wish to be excessively dependent on one external supplier which it does not control. Also there are firms that need powerful processing facilities in addition to CAD, for administration, project management or technical applications like finite element analysis. It is not easy to accommodate different applications on a CAD turnkey system. So in a situation where CAD is the minor application, it may certainly be better to obtain the hardware and software separately.

The dangers of combining CAD and 'number-crunching' activities have already been discussed. The latter must not be permitted to degrade the rapid interactive response of the computer for CAD work. So in the early generations of CAD turnkey systems, isolation of CAD from everything else was put forward as a virtue. However having acquired some experience, many firms with turnkey systems are coming to realise that it is not at all desirable to divorce drawing work from all their other computing activities. In short, the virtue is turning into vice. The solution is not impossible: it is to proportion the processor properly to match the expected load, or to position the processors appropriately in a network.

So purchase of software and hardware separately involves several suppliers. It follows that contracts for supply and maintenance must be set up with each hardware supplier. Later when the system malfunctions, the system manager cannot automatically call up one firm. Instead he must decide whether the problem is likely to lie in one piece of equipment or another, or in the software, and act accordingly.

So this is inevitably a more difficult course, but it can be cheaper than buying from turnkey firms. In addition, a system can be built up which is more closely tailored to individual conditions in the firm. These hardware decisions do need to be made in conjunction with those on the software source, otherwise the software choice would be severely restricted. Indeed the hardware choice should defer to the software selection as already argued.

Obviously the major source of CAD software is the CAD turnkey suppliers, some but not all of whom might be content to sell their software on its own. The software package must be capable of operating on an entirely standard and readily available hardware configuration. Despite the existance of so-called portable high level computer languages, individual CAD software packages normally only operate on one or two types of computer. Where there is a choice, they tend to work best on the computer for which they were designed or with which the software firm is more familiar.

WRITING OR COMMISSIONING WRITING OF SOFTWARE

This is the only course open when the requirements are so specialised that appropriate software is not already available. It would normally be a very expensive solution. There could be a long delay before the product became available. The advantage is that it can be planned and written to fit special requirements, and later on it can be upgraded or further developed to cater for changing needs and ideas.

Sometimes large organisations prefer this solution when they feel that they cannot be dependent on any external supplier for a vital facility. Where the applications knowhow needs to be jealously guarded for commercial or other reasons, the development may have to be done in-house. However writing or specially commissioning CAD software must never be considered lightly because, quite apart from initial costs, its maintenance would represent a huge continuing commitment in future years.

CHAPTER 10

Assessment and Selection of Turnkey Systems

In practice most CAD systems come from turnkey suppliers, and rather fewer as software packages to be run on existing minicomputers. This chapter will deal with the manner in which the study team can set about choosing a turnkey system. It discusses the many points which need to be inquired about. Where software only is sought, then many of the comments on hardware will still have some relevance to the existing equipment.

LIST OF REQUIREMENTS

Our aim should not be to identify the 'best' system on the market, for there is no such thing. Instead it should be to find the one which appears to best match the requirements of the particular office.

The study team must set about making a list of its requirements. This task will seem far from easy at first. Each office would arrive at a unique list, and so it is not possible here to formulate any strict guidelines. However with the combination of a growing understanding of CAD techniques and a more detailed knowledge of the work pattern of the firm, it will become easier. Few firms actually set down such a list in a formal manner. However it is strongly recommended that this should be done. If there is no such list, there is no yardstick against which individual systems can be matched.

At the beginning, the list of requirements need not be too detailed. It is better to try to firm up on the major priorities. The following is a shortlist of some of the items that might appear:

Supplier having knowledge of construction industry
System with construction industry 'feel'
Upgrade potential in hardware
Good drawing efficiency
Three-dimensional modelling (if indeed this is wanted at all)
Supplier active in research and development
Supplier with good reputation and apparent stability
System able to cope with several large projects
Many systems already in use elsewhere
Existing users obviously satisfied with system
Good training facilities
Easy to use

Many facilities in system
Low cost.

This might do for a start. Some of the items might be mutually exclusive, for example a superlative system will not be available at low cost. However this need not concern us too deeply at the start.

There is a case for the emphasis to be on:

Supplier
Software facilities
Hardware features

in that order. The importance of the turnkey supplier and the customer's continuing dependence on him has already been emphasised. The upgrade potential of the hardware ought to be high on most lists, but otherwise much more emphasis ought to be on the capabilities and suitability of the programs rather than on the equipment. There is often an element of choice with the hardware and to some extent a configuration can be designed and assembled to suit the individual firm.

In time, the list of requirements will get more detailed. Systems studied will vary considerably in their properties and capabilities. None may approximate very closely to the firm's ideal. So to make a meaningful comparison in these circumstances it is necessary to look into the *relative* importance of each requirement, and see how each system measures up.

This is best done by deciding on a weighting factor to indicate the relative importance of each item in the list. The values chosen would be based on the organisation's needs and on the preferences of the study team. Armed with this list, the team could then assess each of the shortlisted systems. How each system matches up to each of the requirements could be evaluated in turn and a score in the range of say, 0 to 10 agreed upon. When all items are scored, a simple arithmetical procedure of multiplying each score by its weighting factor and summing would lead to a total score for that system. The system which gets the highest total score would win as it would best match the firm's requirements.

Obviously a low system cost is an item which attracts a high score. In this way it might be possible to come to terms with such alternatives as an expensive system with many features, versus a somewhat cheaper system with fewer features. The use of weighting factors is simpler to use than it appears when explained here, but the list of requirements is obviously the starting point.

POTENTIAL SUPPLIERS AND SHORTLISTS

Now a list of potential suppliers must be created. There are many CAD systems on the market. So the problem is to reduce the list to as few as possible, but without eliminating any system that has winning qualities. This is far from easy. However many of the systems are not used in the construction industry, and perhaps could be safely eliminated on that score alone. The elimination process is more easily and more surely done if the requirements list has been carefully created beforehand. All sources of information, knowledge and advice can contribute including firms already using CAD systems, advice from external consultants, exhibitions, conferences, and of course the potential suppliers themselves. Indeed the requirements list could form the basis of a questionnaire sent to a number of potential suppliers. Use of the list saves time.

A knowledgeable and capable team might well be able to arrive rapidly at a shortlist of between two and four suppliers. This would be ideal. In practice the team might be a lot less confident. A reasonable procedure then would be to get the number down to six or eight, as a first stage. An examination of each of these over a period of time using the list of requirements should enable a reasonable shortlist to be established later on. The process should not be rushed because obviously it would be tragic to miss the supplier of a very suitable system and then find out after another supplier had been given the order.

DEMONSTRATIONS, REFERENCES, VISITS AND DRAWING TESTS

Each of the firms on the shortlist can be approached for a demonstration of its facilities. Given freedom to proceed along well rehearsed lines, such demonstrations will probably be impressive. Furthermore the system demonstrated most recently always seems the best! Use the requirements list to avoid this problem.

It is reasonable that firms should have some freedom in this respect, because they need to demonstrate the capabilities of a necessarily complex system in the most effective manner. But whenever possible, the demonstration should be held using a configuration – hardware and software – that is identical to the one proposed.

Demonstrations using prerecorded sequences are of little value for indicating the procedures of command input and use of the workstation. They often omit time consuming computer operations such as hidden line removal from perspective views, and only display the results. At the vendor's premises, it is very difficult to make a reasonable assessment of response times and computer capacity in a multiterminal system. This is because it is so difficult always to assess the effect of other concurrent processes.

So in addition to giving the supplier full rein for a time, the team should have taken along one or two drawings that are typical of the firm's output. The demonstrators should be quizzed in some detail on how selected features on these drawings would be tackled.

Sometimes an attempt is made to assess the efficiency of systems by supplying a typical drawing or some standard graphical test. Then the supplier is required to input this to the system. This is often timed and is known as a 'benchmark test'. If a large and complex drawing is specially input, this can be a lengthy and expensive process for the vendor. If not very carefully organised and undertaken with a deep knowledge of what is going on, the process is of little real value to the customer. Most systems can cope somehow with most of the content of traditional drawings. Some tests of this kind only use a fairly limited range of system facilities. What is much more important is to find out how effective and how simple it is to use the system overall and how extensive are its facilities.

A simple and useful drawing test would be to ask the supplier to gain access to some previously input drawing which is at least as big and complex as any done currently within the customer's firm. Then they should be asked to make a variety of alterations to this. This can throw some light on the effectiveness of the editing features, and on computer response times when complex tasks are being undertaken.

Much can be gained from visits to firms that have already purchased the system. Normally these are arranged by the supplier. They should be kept as brief as possible since they are always expensive in terms of the time voluntarily given by the host. Obviously the supplier will suggest a visit that is likely to reflect favourably on his interests, and of course no organisation is likely to admit to buying the wrong system. Nevertheless much valuable information can be gained, and it is usually possible to find out if they are truly happy with the system or not. What must be sought is further evidence on the soundness of the supplier, the nature of the work undertaken and what problems have been encountered. Especially useful will be the firm's views on the training process, how often software and hardware faults have occurred, and how effectively they have been dealt with. It is especially important to observe how they are coping with large projects, i.e. projects that have at least the number, size and complexity of drawings as those to be undertaken by the customer. Indeed this may be a surer way than benchmarking of assessing the ability or limitations of the system to cope with sizeable projects.

ASSESSMENT OF SYSTEMS

The systems shortlisted have then to be assessed carefully and in detail over a period of time. Every opportunity should be grasped to learn more about them. In essence what needs to be done is to find out how each system matches up to each of the requirements on the list.

The remaining part of this chapter identifies and discusses the many questions that need answering. This is done under the main headings:

Supplier's organisation
Installed systems
Software: general suitability for purpose
Basic graphics
Editing facilities
Production of drawings
Three-dimensional capability and visualisation
Other features
Software support, maintenance and software enhancements
The workstation
Computer and other hardware.

This can be used as a guide for the study team. It cannot be more than this because circumstances vary so widely.

SUPPLIER'S ORGANISATION

It has been stressed that in practice a contract with a turnkey supplier is a long term agreement. Apart from the supply of equipment and software in the short term, there is training, support, maintenance, and possibly enhancements in the future. It would be a tragedy for the customer, if the turnkey supplier was to fail financially, or was to pull out of this type of business for any reason.

In so far as it is possible for any outsider to check on such matters, it is necessary to determine:

1 How long the firm has been in business
2 The size of the firm
3 Is it increasing in size? If, so, how fast? Does the growth rate appear to be controlled, or headlong and without much control?
4 Are turnover, profit and loss account and balance sheet figures available for recent years? If so, are they healthy? If not, why?

The supplier is in the business of selling a CAD system. It cannot aim at and hope to satisfy all disciplines and industries.

5 Which discipline/industry is it mainly aiming at? Does it have much real knowledge of the customer's business?

If not, the system may at best be a general-purpose draughting system; it may be unsuitable for the customer's longer term needs. The supplier is unlikely to be a source of useful specialised applications software in the future.

6 In what industry did the software itself originate?

Systems that originate in one industry tend to be structured for that type of work and may not be so suitable for other work. Care is necessary here, because many CAD systems have for example originated in electronics or in mechanical engineering. Perhaps the bulk of the supplier's expertise remains in the original field. Then in an attempt to expand their activities, there is a tendency to appoint an architect or civil engineer to the marketing team. Customer dependence on such an individual would be unwise. He may remain in the marketing area, and may not be much in evidence for training, support or development after a contract has been signed.

7 Is the firm the producer and owner of the software, or merely a marketing agent?

An agent may lack depth of understanding of the product. The quality of the support and his ability to maintain the system needs to be questioned closely. At any time in the future, an agent might arbitrarily switch his main interests to another product or activity that is seen as being more profitable.

What would be comforting, if it applies, is a close physical proximity to the supplier and an ability to gain access to the real experts on the system when necessary. Nevertheless, because of geographical location or other considerations, it may be necessary to deal with agents or – what may effectively be the equivalent – with branch offices. Then the quality and robustness of the product, and the directness of the communication channels between agent or branch and originator of the system, take on much significance.

The interests and structure of the potential supplier's firm should be considered:

8 Is this system its sole interest, or is it an important part of its range, or is it merely a rather insignificant part?
9 What are the firm's other interests and activities?
10 Does it have a range of skills at its command?
11 What proportion of staff are involved with various activities such as:

> Research and development
> Maintaining programs
> Dealing with hardware
> Marketing
> Client support and training
> Administration?

12 Does it look as if a very few persons are dealing with all of these?
13 What are the apparent capabilities of the representatives that have been seen?

INSTALLED SYSTEMS

A good motto usually is 'Do not be a first-time buyer'. Of course every successful system has a first customer. He wittingly or unwittingly accepted the greatest risks, and in many instances may well have recouped the greatest benefits. But the risks inherent need to be properly evaluated and accepted. Any CAD system is a complex assemblage of programs and hardware. Many systems have a slightly uncertain start in life but are improved as a result of user comment and experience. Often the system producers are expert computer people but almost inevitably they will lack a depth of understanding of the end uses of the system that they are creating. So feedback from users over a significant period of time is often vital.

1 Is it a new or fairly new product? If so, what are the risks?
2 Has much feedback from actual users had time to take effect?
3 Is it a mature system?

Of course the other danger is that systems rapidly become obsolete and indeed can actually degenerate. Some programs can be modified and added to until they become unmanageable, especially if the basic program structure is not too expert. Often when this happens, it needs to undergo a major revision or rewrite. It is important to try to get some feel or indication of just where the system is in this evolutionary cycle.

4 How many systems have been sold overall, and in the same country? How many users are nearby? How many systems are in similar types of organisations?
5 What is the standing or 'quality' of the users?
6 Is there a users' club? If so, who is the chairman or secretary?

A users' club is some evidence of a willingness to cooperate with users after contracts have been signed to find improved ways of using the system. As already indicated, the users themselves are an important source of ideas and suggestions on improvements. But in many cases it is the initiative of the supplier himself that is needed to get a users' club started. At the very least it indicates some confidence in his product.

The existence of a reasonable customer base is important for several reasons. It indicates first of all that other firms, albeit with different needs and criteria, have vetted the system and have been satisfied. It is a source of references on the standing and capabilities of the supplier's organisation, and of the turnkey system itself. When the supplier has reached the shortlist and enquiries are in the 'serious' category, it may be possible for the supplier to fix up a visit to one of the more suitable of the existing customers. A reasonable size of customer base is some indication that finance, as well as pressure, might exist for further development of the system in the future.

The construction industry is fragmented and teams of firms come together for individual projects. Communications between them of graphical information in digital form will become increasingly necessary in the future. CAD systems are not compatible yet and so it is wise to consider very carefully the systems which potential design partners are now using. It is not wise to be completely out of step in this respect if the end result is the isolation of the firm.

SOFTWARE: GENERAL SUITABILITY FOR PURPOSE

Many suppliers make claims of 3-D capability or even of solid modelling, but do not define what is meant by these terms. The customer may have to investigate.

Three-dimensional capability is likely to be more expensive and make greater demands on the computer processor, and operators may find that it is much more difficult to use. So 3-D working is not necessarily to be preferred, and full 3-D facilities are not necessarily more suitable compared with, say, box geometry capability. The customer must decide.

1 Is it basically a 2-D, box geometry, 3-D, or solid modelling system?
2 Can it cope with a range of these? If so, how easy is it to switch between them on the one project? Is it possible to just add more data to describe the third dimension and details of surfaces into the *same* database, or do you have to restart with a different database?
3 Is the main emphasis on draughting or on modelling of a project?
4 Will it cope equally well with all the types of projects and disciplines for which it is required? For example, if it is primarily a modelling system for buildings, will it cope with site survey plans and contouring?

In choosing a system, the firm may opt either to input 3-D descriptions of all items as blanket cover in case there will be a need for them later on. Alternatively, with a few systems it may opt to selectively include 3-D data for certain limited purposes, such as clash detection, room elevation development or generation of certain types of perspective views. The management implications involved between these limits are very important. Sometimes it has been found that full 3-D input is too laborious. It is occasionally found that systems which are purchased for their 3-D capability are used as 2-D drawing systems in practice. But they may not be fully appropriate or sufficiently flexible for this different purpose. Limited 3-D data extensions to a 2-D drawing system can be a powerful tool for many applications.

Apart from general-purpose drawing work, the feasibility study should have revealed the related activities within the customer's organisation. Such activities might be scheduling, costing, budgeting, stock control, programming and project planning, technical analyses such as finite element work, and many others. In many ways this awareness of related activities can be the most important aspect of the feasibility study.

It may point to the need for specific applications packages in addition to the general-purpose CAD system itself. These other applications may need access to data, or may create data which will appear on, or be associated with, drawings. Then related applications programs may have to be found and installed on the same computer. Some related activities have such a close affinity with drawing work that the CAD package sought would have to include such features as an integral part. Associated data, scheduling and some command language programming capability may need to be studied particularly closely to see if these features could cope with the requirements.

BASIC GRAPHICS

The following are some of the facilities that need to be studied with the view to seeing how far they accord with perceived requirements. It is not just a matter of checking whether or not the system can do something, it is often more important to assess how *easily* it can be done. This is certainly not an exhaustive list and relates mainly to 2-D draughting systems.

Shapes or components	Can the user create, manipulate and store shapes or views of components comprising collections of graphic and text elements? Can these shapes be created from lines, points, symbols, text, and combinations of such

	elements or from other previously created shapes, including items already on the screen?
Lines	How are the following constructed: straight lines, parallel lines, perpendicular lines, lines at specified angles, lines tangential to arcs?
	Is it possible to lengthen or shorten existing lines easily?
	How are triangles, rectangles and regular polygons constructed?
Construction lines	Is there a facility for using construction lines as an aid to geometric construction. These are lines which appear on the graphics screen but which will not be plotted. It ought to be very easy to turn their display on or off.
Points	Is there an ability to automatically find points defined by the intersection of two straight or curved lines, and then to use such points for further geometric construction without the user having to be aware of their coordinates?
	How easy is it to draw circles by a variety of means, for example a circle through three points, given the radius and centre, or given the centre and a tangent? Can an arc be drawn when the centre is well off the screen?
	What about other curves such as parabolas, ellipses, splines, road curves? Are they relevant?
	Can a flowing line be drawn through a number of points?
	Can offsets from curves be drawn?
	Can circular fillets or chamfers be inserted automatically between intersecting lines or curves?
Positioning	How easy is it to draw Cartesian or other types of grids?
	Is it possible to locate a point relative to the global axes, or relative to any local origin?
	Can the user constantly switch between global and relative positioning?
Dimensions input	Is it capable of accepting and storing full size dimensions and coordinates so that, at any later date, the graphical details can be reproduced at any specified scale?
Units	What are the basic units of stored coordinates and angles?
	Can they be changed?
	Can the system cope with metric and imperial input and output, with automatic conversion if required?

Measurement

Is there an ability to measure and display:

Distances between any two indicated points
Coordinates of an indicated point
Angles
Radii
Perimeter
Path length along mixed lines and curves
Areas and centroids of shapes?

Dimensions displayed

Can the system automatically calculate and display dimensions?

Does it produce dimension lines, witness lines, figures and units with justification of text and control over the number of decimal places in values?

Is it possible to dimension, in this way, distances, angles, diameters and radii of circles, lengths of curved lines?

Is there a choice of end marks apart from arrowheads?

How easy is it to change or displace the numbers when required?

Precision

The basic precision with which the graphical data is to be held needs careful investigation. Many systems in use for construction industry applications can maintain a precision of about 1 in 1 000 000. This is adequate for most work since dimensions on a site which is 1 kilometre across can be held accurate to the basic unit of 1 millimetre. However this might not be adequate for large projects or for accurate representation of regional areas and mapping applications. This has been discussed in chapter 6.

Some systems hold coordinates in single precision integer form within the computer and an accuracy of only 1 in 32 000 might be possible. This would be inadequate for most applications. It might mean that components larger than 32 metres either cannot be used, or the dimensional accuracy would not be within 1 millimetre. Certain systems hold individual components in this way, but the location of these within the overall site or project is held to perhaps 1 in 1 000 000.

Parameterised shapes

Can the system generate and store shapes in which key dimensions are variables and are supplied each time the shape is used?

This facility is particularly useful for construction components which come in a variety of

	sizes, examples being windows, air conditioning ducts and pipes.
Manipulation	Is it possible to pick out a shape and move it in translation while maintaining orientation and scale, rotate it about a centre not necessarily within the shape or on the screen, mirror it, and change its scale?
	When a shape is mirrored, the associated text should be mirrored in position as a block, but the individual characters must not be mirrored.
Line styles	How comprehensive is the library of available line styles?
	Apart from solid lines, how easy is it to create dotted, dot and dash, and chain-dotted lines in a variety of thicknesses?
	Does the user have any freedom to create and store for future use his own new line styles, including lines consisting of symbols?
	Is there the freedom to easily change line styles at any time or is this dependent on changing layer etc.?
Text	How comprehensive is the library of character styles?
	How easy is it to change character height, width, font, line thickness at any time?
	Can the user create new character styles and store these?
	Can upper or lower case characters be input from the keyboard?
	Is output possible to the screen and plotter?
	Can the user control the justification of each line left, right or centre in the horizontal direction, and by top, bottom or centre in the vertical direction?
Symbols	Is there a library of symbols that are commonly used in building, civil and services engineering, or other discipline of interest?
	Can the user's organisation add to these symbol libraries?
	Is it possible to retrieve symbols and to control their size and orientation irrespective of drawing size and scale?
Shading and hatching	Is the system capable of hatching areas enclosed by a combination of straight lines and curves, and can this shape itself include islands that must remain unhatched? One practical application of this is the hatching of wall areas in elevation to indicate brickwork, with window spaces present.

A reasonable range of hatching styles should exist and the ability to hatch with symbols, for example to indicate concrete in cross-section, would be useful.

EDITING FACILITIES

Pointing

How effectively can the user indicate and lock on or 'snap' to any existing point, line, text item or detail on the screen?

How is the 'hit' indicated, e.g. by flashing?

Basic editing facilities

Can the user easily and rapidly make changes to shapes that have already been created, or are partly created, without the need for backtracking or anticipation of the need to make some particular edit?

Basic editing manipulations should include moving, copying, deleting, trimming, extending, changing scale, rotating, mirroring about any axis, and changing line or character styles.

When rotating details which include text information, the text should never appear upside-down.

The result of any editing operation should be immediately displayed so that it can be checked.

Protection

Is there a facility to go back and negate the effect of the last instruction?

Is there a checkpoint before any major destructive editing operation is carried out?

These are useful in order to protect the user from serious consequences of his mistakes in editing.

Editing fences

Can the user define an area of interest within a perimeter or 'fence'? This might be a rectangular area, or a closed area bounded by straight lines or perhaps even by a path consisting of any combination of straight lines and curves.

Global editing is the ability to change, move or erase all identical components within the fence in one operation.

Does the system permit selective editing or erasure, for instance of:

Only those components lying entirely within the fence

All components lying either entirely or even partially within the fence

Or of whole components, and those parts of components that are within the fence?

PRODUCTION OF DRAWINGS

Grids

Is it possible to create graphical details and drawings with and without a grid system? Orthogonal grids are nearly always used, whereas skew and polar grids seem to be rarely needed.

Is it possible to create several separate grids with different origins, each set at an angle to one another? This is often needed, for example for different wings of a building, or for separate structures on one site.

Categories

This is a means by which the vast amount of information needed for a project is classified into elements such as doors, partitions, ducts, columns and so on. The concept of 'layers' is often used.

How does this process of classification work in the system?

Can users adopt their own classification systems for individual projects?

Are there an adequate number of categories available? In practice it seems that 50–100 or more categories are useful as a minimum. More than this number would be needed where there is multidiscipline working, especially in building design.

How easy is it to change items from one category to another?

Windowing

How is it possible to home in to, or 'window' in to, a portion of the total graphical database?

Is windowing selective by location, for example to include only an indicated area of a particular floor, or by specifying a scale and centre of interest?

Is there a means of selecting the category or discipline of the graphical information in the window?

Such windowing is necessary for displaying different features on the screen, and for setting up plots.

Drawing creation

If it is possible to create views by a windowing process, is it possible to compose a drawing by interactively positioning one or several such views relative to one another within a drawing frame?

After such assembly, can the user view the result on the screen?

Is it possible to store standard frames including title blocks in a library within the system?

THREE-DIMENSIONAL CAPABILITY AND VISUALISATION

The features and relative merits of 3-D working have been covered already, and clearly the potential customer must give the most serious consideration to his requirements in this respect.

After deciding what type of system it is, a few more points for investigation or thought are:

Drawing efficiency	Will the system permit rapid and effective production of drawings? These are in 2-D and are normally the final product needed.
Modular system	Is the system modular, allowing a start to be made with 2-D working, but permitting a move towards 3-D visualisation or full 3-D working when more familiar with CAD work? Where there is any choice, does the whole project have to be in full 3-D, or is there a much more flexible approach of allowing the user to represent individual components in 2-D or 3-D according to requirements?
Three-dimensional input	Is the model built up from elemental solids such as prisms, cylinders, pyramids and so on? Alternatively, is it created by transforming previously produced 2-D details with added data to describe the third dimension? If the bulk of the work is to be in 2-D, the latter may be preferable. How easy is it to cater for curved surfaces? How are transparent surfaces taken care of?
Visualisation	Is it possible to automatically generate elevations and section views, perspectives and isometrics? What other useful projections are possible? Is it possible to have wire line views speedily produced? Is it possible to have hidden lines and surfaces automatically removed, i.e. without the operator having to trim lines? If so, how efficient is the process and what limitations are there? Can lines of interpenetration be automatically generated? How easy is it to change the viewpoint, direction of view and scale? What about half-tones or colour filling? Has the system got the capacity to create

reasonably complex views of the type envisaged?

Is it possible to rapidly switch between say a plan view and a section through a building?

Is it possible to display two or more views simultaneously on one split screen or on separate screens?

Can 3-D views be combined with other views to form a drawing?

Is it possible to generate a perspective view automatically and then to manipulate it as a 2-D drawing? There are opposing views on the merits of this, but it is one way of rapidly adding detail such as humans, cars, trees and such items held in libraries. Most perspective views need to be worked up manually by a skilled artist to make them really presentable.

OTHER FEATURES

Associated non-graphic data

Is it possible to input and store non-graphic data? If so:

How easy is it to handle the input and to manipulate text and numbers?

How easy is it to change the information already held?

How easy is it to change the form of the associated data for different types of components?

Can the system automatically keep a record of the number of instances in which a component is repeated?

How flexible and easy to use are the sorting and report producing facilities? These are vital if the system is to be used to create schedules and parts lists. Useful features of reporting are the ability to control the order, spacing, arithmetic manipulation and summations of columns. Can the user input headings and control pagination?

Programming

Are there any facilities for the user to string together regularly recurring commands into a program?

If so, what features are there in the programming language, for example for jumps and loops in the coding?

How easy would it be to use?

How efficient would it be in operation?

Multiuser working and security

From a consideration of the volume of drawing work to be undertaken, how many workstations does the supplier propose? Perhaps this number will be limited by the amount of money available.

Can the software support multiuser working simultaneously? Even if only one workstation seems necessary, there may well be a need in the future for more.

Does the software allow more than one person to work on the same project at the same time? If so, how does this work in practice?

Is there a security arrangement, perhaps controlled by the system manager, to prevent for example an architect changing structural details, or a services engineer moving a window position?

Interfaces with external programs

Are there facilities for extracting data from the drawing database, say into a computer file with a specified format, so that the data is readily available for use by an external application program? An example of this may be the extraction of graphical data for a finite element analysis.

Are there facilities for the reverse process? An example here might be the transfer of a table of survey point coordinates from an external program into the drawing database so that the points can be plotted and/or tabulated.

Is there a need for an interface with a specific applications software, such as a road design package?

Open ended systems may not seem important initially, but this aspect is likely to increase in importance as computer applications become more coordinated and integrated.

Communication with other CAD systems

Other organisations with whom there is some association may be operating another CAD system.

Is there any requirement to pass drawings in digital form? If so, are there special interface programs available so that data can be passed from one system to the other, and vice versa? It may be that only the elementary items such as lines, arcs and characters are transferred with no higher level structure. Then it is difficult to interactively modify the received drawing.

Do both systems conform to the IGES Standard? Initially this standard only covers 2-D drawings.

Specialist applications software	The first CAD package obtained may well be a good general-purpose draughting or modelling system. Needs are likely to develop for specialist applications programs. Examples might be in concrete or steel detailing or in environmental analysis. Apart from the product under consideration, what other applications software is currently available from the supplier? What is currently being developed? If relevant to the customer's needs, at what stage is the development work?

SOFTWARE SUPPORT, MAINTENANCE AND SOFTWARE ENHANCEMENTS

Documentation	The quality of system documentation is usually, but not always, a guide to the quality of the system itself. Documentation falls into categories of marketing brochures, training manuals and reference manuals. What is the quality and sufficiency of the last two categories? As system documentation is often bulky, its organisation, layout and indexing need to be assessed.
Training	The supplier will usually include a specified number of his staff's man-days for training and instruction of a reasonable number of the customer's personnel. How many days and how many staff? It might be prudent to check on who would actually undertake the training and whether they could adequately relate to the customer's staff and their requirements.
User support	Customer support is partly an extension of the initial training, namely getting the user out of difficulties of his own making. But there may also be problems caused when the system fails because of program bugs. Obviously a system which other users have found to be reliable, reasonably easy to use, and robust is of considerable advantage. Periodic updates, perhaps two per year, are one means by which a supplier can eliminate minor bugs and also make improvements to the efficiency and capabilities of his system. The supplier will usually be keen to supply these as he will have

no wish to maintain different software versions at different sites.

What is the supplier's capability to undertake this work?

How many staff does he have engaged in this role and how does this relate to the number of systems installed?

Where are the support staff located in relation to the customer's offices?

It is rather important that all such upgrades are totally compatible with the old drawing databases. If system improvements do necessarily involve a change of database structure, then conversion programs and procedures that are simple to apply must be supplied.

Major upgrades

Upgrades in software capabilities might be a different matter.

Often these are structured as optional modules to provide for example 3-D viewing or colour facilities. Alternatively they may be compatible applications packages such as architectural scheduling or steel detailing. Usually these are not included in the normal maintenance.

The user may in time find that they are both highly desirable and highly expensive.

What constitutes a minor upgrade included in the normal maintenance contract, and what becomes a separately priced module, may be far from clear. Attitudes of different suppliers vary. Perhaps the only guide to the future is to examine the supplier's past record in this respect.

OPERATION WORKSTATION

Input of drawing data

Is interactive input of data the normal method, with graphical detail displayed immediately it is input? This facilitates the constant checking for errors, and then corrections can be done immediately.

How informative are the system prompts displayed when information is required from the operator?

Can the operator reduce the quantity of prompt information when he becomes more familiar with the commands?

Are there facilities for calling for help from the program itself when he gets into difficulties?

How advanced is the system at checking for errors made by the operator?

How informative are the warning and error messages?

Note that the bulk of the time will be spent inputting graphical information and these aspects are important.

Method of input

Is input done by means of commands and parameters typed in at the keyboard, by using screen or digitiser menus, using function keys or by some combination of these methods?

Can the individual user choose between different methods available, i.e. choosing the most convenient for the task in hand?

Can he easily switch between the options?

Ergonomic arrangement of workstation

There was a time when users were lucky to have any facilities for interactive drawing and they had to adapt to what was available. This time is now past. The operators have to work effectively and rapidly for relatively long periods.

Are the workstations well designed and comfortable to use?

Is there plenty of adjustment available in the positions and angles of the individual elements?

Is there plenty of room to lay out reference drawings and other documents?

Some workstations have been carefully designed with the user in mind, others are merely cobbled together.

Screens

What types are available?

What is the size and resolution?

Do they have to accommodate screen menus as well as commands, parameters and user prompts?

Are they monochrome, and if so which colour is it?

Are multicolour operations possible and worth the extra money?

A few terminals, designed for handling documents rather than project drawings, have the rectangular screens turned in portrait rather than landscape orientation. This seems rather unsatisfactory.

Are refresh screens going to be free from flicker even when moderately complex drawings are displayed at all terminals?

How would the screens cope in strong drawing office lighting?

| | How far can the workstations be from the computer? |
| Mixed types of workstation | Some systems permit a choice of workstation types. Consideration might then be given to obtaining some high quality terminals for the more accomplished operators, and cheaper ones for others, for training, for quick look-ups, and for inputting and manipulating non-graphic information. |

COMPUTER AND OTHER HARDWARE

Processor and memory	Who makes the computer? Exactly which model, and how much memory is proposed? Is the computer a standard model, which is readily available from the manufacturer also, or is the hardware or operating system specially designed or modified to run the CAD system? Is it a single user type of system, or a multiterminal type? If the latter, what is the maximum number of workstations that can be dealt with efficiently? Which other firm operates this number already? To operate this maximum number, would additional memory or disc capacity be necessary?
Disc storage	What type of discs are proposed? Are the discs exchangeable? After being shown some drawings typical of the customer's output, can the supplier predict the number of drawings that could be held simultaneously on the disc? How will the discs be backed up for security? How long will it take? What will be the means of long term archiving of drawings in digital form?
Magnetic tape	Will a magnetic tape be included in the configuration? If so, what is the speed and density of writing and reading information?
Plotter	What type and model is proposed? Will it be possible to plot drawings simultaneously with use of all the workstations? Can a number of drawings be queued up within the computer for plotting? How long will it take to plot a drawing typical of the customer's output in ink (also in ball point etc) when all workstations are in use? How much spare capacity will there be? How many pens are there?

	What media can be used? What about drawing frames and title blocks?
Digitiser	For the type of applications envisaged, will a large digitiser be necessary?
Hard copy	Particularly if one or more workstations are remote from the plotter, or the plotter is likely to be fairly busy, there may be a need for one or more hard-copy units.
Printer	What provision is being made for printing of tabular information such as schedules or bills of materials?
Remote workstations and communication	Are there any special provisions to be made for terminals at remote sites, or for linking separate workstations or computers together? If so, how will this be done, and how will it operate?
Hardware upgrade path	It is important to look beyond the configuration being proposed; this cannot be stressed too much. What are the various means and current costs of increasing the capacity of the system?
Accommodation for hardware	What space and environmental conditions are necessary for the equipment, and what arrangements must be made?
Hardware maintenance	What is known about reliability of the proposed equipment? How often do failures occur? Who will provide the hardware maintenance – the turnkey supplier or the computer manufacturer?

CHAPTER 11

Financial and Legal Considerations of System Acquisition

The supplier will have a document which sets out his standard terms and conditions of business. A copy normally will be included with his quotation or tender.

It is reasonable to expect that in some instances this document will favour the supplier. So, although it may form the basis of a contract, the buyer should not automatically accept all the conditions as proposed. He must study them carefully, possibly with professional legal advice, and must strike out or rewrite all conditions which seem to be unsatisfactory. Many suppliers will be prepared to renegotiate such items until a fair and equitable agreement is reached. If not, and the disagreement is serious, then the buyer must look elsewhere.

This chapter describes some of the financial arrangements and contract conditions that normally apply.

ACQUIRING SYSTEMS

Options might be to purchase, lease or rent. The choice depends on individual circumstances.

Purchase means that the buyer obtains full legal title to the equipment. He may be able to claim tax allowances or government grants. Also he can generally depreciate the equipment in the most advantageous way. At any time he can sell the equipment to another party. Purchasers sometimes find it inconvenient to have to provide the cash for the full system cost at the outset.

With leasing arrangements, the customer avoids having to find the full system price at the start. Instead payment is a revenue item over the set period of the lease. After that time, payment is normally at a negligible rate, but title never actually passes to the customer. No capital allowances or grants can be claimed by him. The leasing company may be able to claim these, however, and if so this ought to be reflected in its rates.

Rental may be an option. A short term commitment could permit the user to try out the system without incurring serious obligations. It provides scope for upgrading at intervals with the latest technology. Rates are likely to be high, however, especially for short periods, because of the costs of implementation and training.

The above paragraphs apply to hardware. The situation regarding software is normally rather different. Normally the source code is not supplied, nor is the software sold outright. This is because the supplier wishes to retain full title to the software himself, so that he can supply it to other parties in the same manner in the future. What is offered normally is a non-exclusive licence for the customer to use the software. This might be for use in perpetuity, for a set period, or on an annual basis. The first is somewhat similar to, but not legally the same as, outright purchase. Normally the buyer will not be able to modify the software, to sell it, or perhaps even to allow any third party to use it. When a system is leased, some finance companies might not be prepared to lease that portion of the system cost that relates to the software. This is because of its intangible nature and their interest in holding collateral for the outstanding monies.

CONTRACT CONDITIONS

In the UK the Institute of Purchasing and Supply has produced model conditions for purchasing and for maintenance of computer systems. These can be used as a guide as to what is normal, fair and reasonable.

The contract is a legal document which sets out the rights of the supplier and customer. It also details the responsibilities of each party and is an attempt to foresee and provide for as many eventualities as possible.

The hardware and software must be adequately described. For the hardware, the description can be in the form of a schedule of items. The manufacturer, model and capacities of each element are listed so that all are uniquely detailed. Software is often in modular form and may exist in various versions. If there are several elements, then again these ought to be listed in a schedule. The software is more difficult to describe specifically, but the customer must be clear about precisely what is being offered.

Generally the supplier's quotation will be a fixed price valid for a period of perhaps 30 days from its date. The amount of any taxes payable should be detailed. The total should include all costs of shipping, normal delivery, installation, training, documentation and other items as set out in the contract. It is probable that hardware and software maintenance will be excluded and be subject to a separate agreement.

The price of imported items may be liable to change with currency fluctuations. The supplier might reserve the right to impose a surcharge if the fluctuation moves against him by more than a specified amount.

Payment terms must be clearly stated. They may be specified as percentages due respectively on order, on delivery and on acceptance. There may be a percentage retention for a specified period after acceptance. This is desirable from the purchaser's point of view.

A delivery date should be agreed and specified. The cost of delivery of hardware and software would normally be included in the price, or detailed separately. But what is meant by delivery? If any surcharges will be imposed for moving the hardware within the customer's premises to its final required position, then the customer ought to be made aware of this beforehand. Risks are normally borne by the supplier until the items enter the customer's premises. It follows that the customer must arrange to be covered by his own insurance from that moment on. The customer must be aware of and agree on any penalties that would be imposed on him if he should be the cause of any delay in the agreed delivery schedule, for example because accommodation for the equipment is not ready. Similarly the supplier's obligations in this respect, if the system or some component is delivered late, should be clear. Sometimes the supplier merely agrees to use reasonable endeavours to comply with the agreed delivery data and accepts absolutely no further responsibilities in the matter.

Curiously, some suppliers expect the customer to check the delivery and to notify any omissions, losses or damages within a specified short period. Clearly the customer is not well qualified to undertake such a duty. It would be unwise to accept such responsibility or indeed to make any move himself to unpack delivered equipment.

Soon after the hardware is installed and commissioned, the software will be loaded from magnetic media and stored in the computer. Then some system acceptance tests will be carried out in the presence of the customer. These tests should be scheduled in the contract and the customer should ensure that these cover a wide range of the software features. Also they must include the operation of all the hardware devices, including all workstations and the plotter, as well as digitisers, hard-copy units and remote communications facilities if supplied. The customer might prefer to have the system proved to his satisfaction over a longer period, but perhaps this is the purpose of having a percentage retention.

The customer's rights to the software, or rather the limitations being imposed on him, will be specified in some detail. Usually it is in the form of a licence for the customer's organisation and its employees to use the software on one processor at an agreed site. This will be for a specified period or for the period of the agreement. The contract will probably state that no title, copyright or other rights of a proprietary nature pass to the customer. An additional fee payable in the future if the software is required to be operational on other machines might be set out. This can be particularly important, and indeed may be a serious limitation in the future if the system is to be upgraded and as the concept of distributed processing takes hold.

The supplier will usually include clauses which require the user firm and its employees to keep secret and confidential the information, techniques and knowhow associated with the program. The user may not be permitted to sublicense the use of the programs to third party organisations. If the user acts in the manner of a computer bureau and wishes to permit other firms to use the program on his computer, then additional royalties on such use might be payable. A reasonable analogy is that the customer is permitted to operate a 'laundry' but not a 'launderette'. There may be a clause which prohibits any modifications from being made to the program, although without the source code this may be difficult anyway.

The supplier may give a software warranty to the effect that he will correct any software errors that are detected by users. Unfortunately he may be unwilling to place a time scale on the corrective measures. Also there almost certainly will be a clause which expresses his limitation to liability for any consequential damages arising from software failures.

Documentation supplied should be itemised and this ought to include user reference manuals and training manuals. Documentation is expensive to produce and the number of copies included in the price should be stated. The price of additional copies should be known.

The system price will usually include a stated number of man-days for training and instruction of a reasonable number of the user's personnel. Clearly it is important to find out if this will be adequate, and to determine the cost of additional man-days in case these are needed.

It is worth having a clause included which states that the supplier will maintain a copy of the source code and appropriate documentation in a safe deposit at specified premises other than the supplier's offices. The exceptional event of the supplier becoming incapable of maintaining the software can occur. So this clause ought to be framed so as to provide some safeguard to enable the customer to make other arrangements if this happens.

The above are the main items which have specific relevance to turnkey contracts. There will in addition be some general clauses of the type that might be found in most contracts. Examples include clauses dealing with the period of the agreement, conditions for terminating the agreement, procedures for giving notices, procedures for arbitration, and waivers. The governing law will be stated.

MAINTENANCE

Hardware may be warranted in a turnkey contract for a period of perhaps 90 days. It is important to appreciate what conditions apply. In particular some hardware manufacturers limit such warranties to the rectification of faults or replacement of parts but only if the equipment is returned to the factory. In practice this is of little or no benefit to most users. In such circumstances the user is effectively forced to enter into a hardware maintenance contract from the date of acceptance.

Usually maintenance is undertaken on an annual basis and so may be the subject of a separate agreement. The conditions vary considerably. Turnkey organisations are usually not the actual manufacturers of the hardware so they may not have any ability to maintain it themselves. Then they may act as an agent for the customer. They in turn may enter into contracts with the hardware suppliers. Alternatively the turnkey firm may merely organise some contracts between the customer and ultimate suppliers. The former is to be preferred. Then the onus for isolating a fault to one hardware supplier does not devolve on the customer – who may not have the experience to cope.

Firms normally undertake to respond to a service call during specified office hours and within say eight working hours, i.e. within one working day, of the call. A faster response might be agreed upon for a higher charge. Such emergency calls would be in addition to routine visits of specified frequency for preventive maintenance measures. Routine visits should be arranged well beforehand.

Hardware maintenance should be cheaper during the first year because of the warranties. At the time of ordering, it may be rather difficult to obtain a quotation for the second and subsequent years. Then there is inevitably some latent fear that future maintenance charges for 'old' items will be progressively increased. This could tend to force the customer into replacing items before their useful life has expired simply because they become prematurely too expensive to maintain. The subject of upgrades and system enhancements was discussed in chapter 8.

Software maintenance, support for users and periodic upgrades are normally included in the annual maintenance contract.

CHAPTER 12
Management

NEED FOR PREPARATION

Management of the CAD system must start early on, indeed as soon as the order has been signed. No CAD system will manage itself. Whatever the potential benefits, the greatest pitfall is that there will be inadequate preparation and little ongoing management. The problem can arise simply because the top people in the organisation are so deeply involved in the selection and decision making process. When the order has been signed, they sometimes feel that their active role is finished, and others will take over. Perhaps they feel that it is entirely the province of the turnkey supplier. Then after the large investment of time and money, there is the danger that frustration and disappointment sets in.

It need not, and indeed it must not, happen like this. The coming of a CAD system may initiate fundamental changes in an organisation, and in such a situation the firm's management must lead. It is a serious business.

HUMAN ELEMENT

As in many other fields of management, it is the human element that needs to be stressed. A CAD system is not automatic. It needs human beings to operate it, and they will determine whether it is a success or otherwise.

Most innovations lead to fears and uncertainties before their appearance. It is understandable if there are even fears of unemployment in some quarters, since CAD is usually introduced expressly with the aim of increasing productivity. Yet the activities in which the CAD system excels, the routine drawing of components, copying them, making alterations to existing drawings, and scheduling, are the types of work that draughtsmen find boring and tedious. This is what prevents young people taking up this career, or what drives off those already in it to more interesting jobs when they get the chance. There is probably a shortage of suitable draughtsmen in many places, and there certainly will be as economic activity picks up to a degree. For designers, a CAD system offers the prospect of a greater proportion of time available for their creative activities. It could be argued that the staff in those firms that are prepared to invest in CAD will have rather less to fear from the perils of local and international competition than others. It is important, however, that staff are kept fully informed of, and perhaps permitted to take some part in, the studies, decisions and preparations.

WHO SHOULD MANAGE AND WHO SHOULD USE THE SYSTEM?

Only those people who can draw on drawing boards now, and who can create useful drawings already, should even try to use a CAD system. Also, the amount of computer expertise required, although certainly not negligible, should not be overrated. These assertions are made in the belief that it would be much easier to train a competent draughtsman in the necessary computing skills than to train a computer person in any of the disciplines of the construction industry.

Other than in exceptional circumstances it is not necessary, and indeed may be counter-productive, to set up a computer department to run the system. Any existing data processing staff may not be particularly knowledgeable about CAD or its management. They can be expected to have little understanding of drawing office procedures. In most circumstances, therefore, the CAD facilities need to be managed and staffed by drawing office people.

CAD brings a whole set of new management problems. The management patterns are not yet fully established, or even well understood. But it is vital that one person is selected to coordinate activities or be in charge, and if possible this should be done before the equipment is delivered. Some firms may prefer to have an architect or engineer to oversee the system. Except with very large systems, this can be a part time activity. Indeed it is important that he does not become totally immersed with the computer – it is after all only a very powerful tool. It is better if he can remain involved at least to some extent in his existing discipline, respected by his peers with whom he will have to liaise, and he needs a flexible and enthusiastic frame of mind. Some firms might prefer the existing chief draughtsman or some equivalent. The chosen person does not need to already possess any special computer knowledge, but the supplier firm must attend to this within its training programme. He must be willing to learn.

Attributes required for the users are traditional draughting skill, enthusiasm for new techniques, an ability to perservere to overcome early difficulties and a modicum of intelligence. The organisation and each user will have to invest resources in the learning process. Clearly both parties to the agreement should be able to see some benefits ahead.

During the system selection process, it will have been noted that some systems are better for design, and others better for drawing production. Some are easy to use but might be shallow; others might be more difficult because there are so many facilities available. So whether the system ordered should be taken up by designers who might prefer to use it intermittently when their projects require it, or by full time draughtsmen for intensive use, is clearly something that has to be thought about during system selection. It will of course guide operator selection.

As a generalisation, it does seem that architects prefer to do most of their drawing work themselves, rather than to delegate it to draughtsmen. They do their 'design' by drawing. So it is possible that many architects, even those in senior positions, may wish to use the CAD system themselves. Engineers on the other hand are more likely to look upon the drawing process as record making. They perform the design, and calculations form a part of this process. They then try to save their own time by having a draughtsman to record the details of their work.

Whatever is decided, it is best to maintain as flexible a view as possible, and to be prepared to modify the plan where, in the light of some experience, it proves necessary. Fixed ideas, such as the system being only for technicians, only for professionals, or indeed for any set of persons, should not be allowed to gain ground.

ACCOMMODATION FOR EQUIPMENT

Arrangements for accommodating the equipment, and many other necessary preparations, must all be completed in good time. There is little sense in paying for an expensive system, only to have it lying idle for a time. The supplier should advise on all the environmental requirements and other items, which might include some of the following:

Power supply
Temperature
Humidity
Cleanliness of air
Noise from cooling fans, printers, plotters, etc.
Lighting, especially at workstations
Layout of equipment, including maintenance access
Cable runs for terminals
Telephone lines for data communication, if relevant
Static electricity
Fire/smoke detection
Access (or restriction of access) to equipment
Storage space for consumables, e.g. paper, tapes.

As already indicated, the modern computer system is far less demanding in many of these respects compared with its predecessor. This is especially true of small systems. The supplier or firm that is going to maintain the equipment may well wish to agree on the arrangements in advance.

It usually makes sense to accommodate all the equipment, except the workstations, in one room where the environment can be controlled. In general, people would not work there but would need access from time to time, for example to take drawings off the plotter. Ideally a glass door or window should permit the progress of plotters or printers to be observed from outside.

A policy on location of workstations needs to be decided. They can be either dispersed within the drawing offices, or grouped together in one zone. Arguments for dispersal are that the CAD facility might be more readily integrated and accepted within the firm's day-to-day business. Also the users do not have to gather all their reference material together and transport it at the start of each session. Counter-arguments for grouping them together are that this encourages users to prepare more carefully for sessions. They are less likely to be disturbed during sessions, and it is easier for them to cooperate together, discuss difficulties and share knowledge. Sometimes it is found that designers from different disciplines in a firm only ever begin meeting and understanding one another when they come to use the workstations. It is likely to be easier to arrange suitable lighting for workstations if they are not to be used within the brightly lit drawing office.

TRAINING

Training of the initial batch of users is usually undertaken by the supplier after the system has been installed and commissioned. It can be argued that this is too late. Time can be gained if they can be trained at the supplier's premises, at a bureau or perhaps at another firm which is operating the same system already. Such off-site training saves the expense of maintaining an otherwise idle system during the initial training period, and there may be other financial benefits in speeding up the system introduction. These benefits may sometimes compare favourably with the extra costs involved in off-site training. But such training must then be held immediately prior to delivery, and must never be provided too early.

When training is started, each user must be encouraged to work intensively at it, and preferably for about 50% of his working time. Two users can be trained together at each terminal, one operating and the other watching and 'advising'. Then at intervals their roles can be switched. Certainly well within a week or so, they should be encouraged to start working on real project drawings.

Even if user training is done after delivery, serious consideration ought to be given to providing some training earlier on, at least for the system manager. It is quite important that he keeps ahead of the others, and can establish himself early in an advisory role. Most suppliers do not pay enough regard to the specialist training needed by the manager.

Adequate attention is rarely given to refresher courses or advanced training for users. After three to six months, users are often fairly confident and reasonably effective. But they adopt fixed work procedures and they are not always aware of or using some of the more advanced features of the system. This is the time when a small amount of additional training can be invaluable.

There is likely to be a need later on to bring in and train new users. This may be after the supplier's training obligations are completed. It should perhaps be one function of the manager, or of one or two of the main users, to organise such further training.

In the early days and weeks, the users will be under much stress. They will be under the spotlight, and everyone will be interested in demonstrations, and in seeing some results! Their existing and unrelated workload will continue to provide its normal crop of problems. But too much should not be expected too early. The firm's management must try to shield them as much as possible during this initial period. This is just when most patience is needed by all. After all, these people did not learn to draw with pencil and paper in a few days. Systems vary in this respect, as do individuals, but it may well require a few weeks before they have gained a speed comparable with their manual methods, and perhaps three months or more before they are operating at full speed. Throughout this time, and afterwards until full confidence is gained by all concerned, no attempt should be made to dispose of apparently unwanted conventional drawing boards.

OPERATIONS

The ratio of cost of CAD equipment to that of a draughtsman is falling rapidly. But it has not yet fallen so far that the workstation costs can be regarded too lightly by management. The equipment must be used intensively. This means two things in many organisations. First, no user should be allowed to adopt a workstation as his personal asset; each must be shared by several operators. Secondly, some form of shift working or at least flexible working hours may have to be instituted so as to squeeze as many equipment working hours as possible into each day. It is best for at least the principles to be established before the system is delivered and before the first users are selected. This way there are likely to be fewer misunderstandings.

Workstation sessions always need to be planned in advance and rotas drawn up and maintained. Two or three hour-long sessions seem to be best since operator efficiency undoubtedly starts to decline after that time. Users will need to gather information and plan their session before they start, and then adhere closely to agreed schedules. Interruptions including telephone calls should definitely be discouraged or even banned. In practice firms vary considerably in the degree of flexibility allowed, But the firms and operators that appear to fare the best are those that establish and get used to operating a fairly rigid regime of rotas.

One of the system manager's duties is to decide, or at least advise, on the type of work which is best suited for CAD, and to determine priorities. He will soon build up some experience in this. In principle, the greatest benefits lie in drawing work where there are:

1 Many repetitions of details
2 Many people interested in the information
3 Alterations likely later on
4 Bills of materials or schedules required in addition to drawings (assuming the system can produce these).

It could be said that item 3 above results from item 2. Usually the benefits are greater when CAD is used on large projects, although this is not an argument for not using it on quite small jobs. Some examples of suitable drawings are:

1 General arrangement drawings on which much of the basic information is repeated and used by different disciplines, e.g. grids, building outlines, structural outlines, key plans, staircases, lift cores.
2 Plans or elevations with elements repeated, perhaps at different scales on different drawings, such as cladding panels, brick details, ceiling plans.
3 Drawings that reappear in different guises during the life of the project, such as outline design drawings which are worked up into tender drawings, then construction drawings, and finally modified to form construction record drawings.
4 Bar charts used for planning. Arguably these are changed more frequently than any other drawings.

Early on, some consideration should be given to establishing rules for a 'house style' for the office. A CAD system can enable management to exercise some control over this fairly easily. This may merely involve some conventions for character sizes and styles, line widths and styles, a library of standard symbols, and the setting up of standard title blocks for drawings. If required, it could involve much more, to include for example standard notes for drawings and the format of schedules.

Each user must always be on the lookout for shapes or components created which could be reused later, albeit by his colleagues, on other projects and perhaps after some modification. The system manager will need to work out naming strategies for such items which can be kept in libraries within the system. When creating names, a balance must be struck between brevity and longer, more descriptive names, bearing in mind that errors tend to increase rapidly with an increase in the key strokes necessary.

A strategy will also have to be worked out by the system manager for the use within the firm of layering techniques, or component categories. This is especially important where multidiscipline teams use the system. A system based on the CI/Sfb classification is often used by architects. Some flexibility needs to be built in to this for coping with special features on drawings and for individual projects.

The efficiency of a system can be increased if it can be tailored more closely to particular needs with high level menus or by use of a command language. All users do not have to work at this level, but one or two of the more able ones certainly should be trained and encouraged in this respect. The importance of this is likely to become more and more apparent as the firm's experience of CAD grows.

The ease with which drawings can be amended has been described as an important benefit. This is indeed usually true, but in the absence of some care it can become a danger. Control of revisions is as important as ever. Operators must not be permitted to make alterations which are outside their mandate. When several people are working on the same project, the layering or category feature can assist because the categories over which each operator has jurisdiction can be defined. He must not alter anything else. The powerful operating systems of the supermini computers provide a first line defence against unauthorised persons gaining access to information. Additionally drawing information can be secured in such a way that one defined operator only can write data at any given time even if several users may be able to examine it simultaneously. Much tighter control may of course be necessary on some project work, such as defence projects or projects which are sensitive for commercial or other reasons.

The disc store of the computer must be 'backed up' regularly. This is the process of copying the contents of the disc to some other permanent storage media. It provides security against failure of the disc, or of accidental loss or corruption of its contents. If anything untoward happens, the worst then is that the work done on the computer since the last back-up is lost, but nothing before that time. Back-up can be either be to some form of removable disc or to magnetic tape, depending on the equipment available. Tape is cheaper but the operation may take longer each time. The back-up copy must be kept other than in the computer room so that drawing data is not lost in the event of a fire. With regard to frequency of back-ups, some balance needs to be struck between risk of loss of data and the effort involved in doing each back-up. Daily or twice weekly are possibilities. However a procedure must be decided on and adhered to rigidly, because a false sense of security tends to be built up over a period by seemingly reliable equipment.

When drawing data held on the disc for some project is no longer active, the data is 'archived' by copying it to a removable disc or magnetic tape. Then the copy of the data can be cleared from the active disc and the space reused for current projects. Archiving can also be done at significant times during the life of a project, such as at the tender stage, or before some major change is made. This means that a frozen copy of the design can be kept very easily. In practice, two archive copies must be taken at each time in case one is subsequently found to be unreadable for some reason. These copies must be stored in separate locations. This stored data is not in completely permanent form and could of course be corrupted if stored in the vicinity of strong magnetic fields or in other unsuitable conditions. Advice needs to be taken regarding normal shelf life and new copies made occasionally.

After a few months or years of operation, the value of the drawing data held becomes immense; hence the importance of proper back-up and archival procedures.

Firms must continue to retain copies of all their important drawings as paper negatives or microfilm in the conventional manner. Sometimes archived drawings are kept for decades. This is a long time in computer terms and it would be extremely unwise to depend totally on future programs being able to interpret the current database structures.

The manager needs to regularly monitor the performance of the system and the work done using it. This helps with the forward load predictions. If the system appears likely to become grossly overloaded, then consideration needs to be given to upgrading in good time. Lead times for additional equipment can be several months.

Some junior person might be needed at least in a part time capacity to look after a pen plotter, especially if it is used fairly intensively. It is also important that someone has the duty of regularly checking stocks of consumable items such as pens, and paper for plotters, toner for electrostatic plotters and so on. It is also necessary to check that preventive maintenance work is being carried out at the agreed regular intervals.

DRAWING MANAGEMENT

The maintenance of up-to-date drawing registers has always been a tedious chore in most firms. However the computer is well able to maintain such registers, provided a suitable program exists. In practice, comparatively few CAD system suppliers appear to provide such facilities.

What is required is the ability to store items such as the drawing reference, author, title, date, size, location, relevant parts number, magnetic tape number and date archived, and so on. The needs of every organisation tend to differ somewhat in detail. It is a database type of program which is needed, but it must be easy to use and must be specially tailored to this particular application. There must be an ability to input, modify, delete and display records of drawings. Facilities must be provided to cope with drawing revisions. It must be possible for example to print all those drawings in the form of a register that matches some selection criteria specified by an enquirer. For example he might want a list of all the drawings for a particular project produced by one author between two specified dates. A list of archived drawings in drawing reference order, with title, archive date and magnetic tape number, might be required on another occasion.

Any such system for drawing registers needs to be open ended so as to permit its use also for manually produced drawings. This is simply because few organisations convert to CAD for 100% of their drawing work. In any case, their main problem lies now with their existing large stock of drawings produced in the conventional manner.

A register system relates to existing drawings. But problems exist also with keeping records of the issue of drawings to other organisations, and with the receipt of drawings from elsewhere. Big organisations even have major problems with internal distribution. Keeping track of when and where particular revisions of each drawing went to is often very tedious, yet is important.

Yet another record keeping problem exists in drawing office management itself. This too can be assisted with a suitable program. The manager's problem is to keep track of all the drawings that will be required for each project. He needs to know who within the office is doing each one, how many hours he has allocated for it, how many of these are used up at any given time, and what is the current percentage completion of each drawing. It is then a simple exercise for a computer to provide the manager from time to time with a summary of the progress of each project. Each drawing in fact is then regarded as a separate task or activity. There appears to be a need for a simple management system of this type, which does not involve the complications of using the full network analysis techniques.

CHAPTER 13
Final Thoughts

We have seen that CAD is not a single uniform technique that can be acquired and integrated into any design organisation with extreme ease. For it is a technique which means different things to different people. As with an onion, we can strip away successive layers to expose different features, capabilities, applications and opportunities.

There are applications in many industries and disciplines. Within the construction industry it is already successfully used by several professional firms, contracting organisations, government departments, local authorities and others. Civil, structural and building services engineers, as well as architects, have found diverse applications, and quantity surveyors are increasingly using its ability for handling project information.

It can be simply an aid to the production of a single drawing, like an electronic pen. But we have seen how graphical information can be created and manipulated to produce some of, or perhaps all, the drawings required for a project. Indeed many systems provide a layering facility so as to permit information for drawings to be classified and handled more effectively.

The graphical data can be efficiently assembled and manipulated as two-dimensional information, and this is the closest approximation to traditional drawing office procedures. This is a perfectly valid procedure that has and will continue to have its adherents. It is also possible by one means or another for the physical project and its solid objects to be described with an element of the third dimension.

Just as a project design develops in the fourth dimension of time, so the CAD model of the project and its drawings can evolve over time. The construction industry is of course particularly prone to design modifications. We have seen that a principal benefit of CAD is the relative ease with which such modifications can be made at all stages of a project.

We have also seen how some systems can cope with non-graphical information – the descriptors, attributes, quantities, costs and so on. The graphics and such attribute data, plus the linkages between them, become a powerful aid to project design, and to the management of the construction phase. This ability to combine and cope with both types of information in fact means that a CAD system can become the nucleus of a project file – the repository of all up-to-date design information for a project during its inception, planning and construction phases.

Most design organisations deal with several projects simultaneously, and this is yet another layer to consider. The ability for information and details used on one project to be utilised on another is something that can really be made to work. Standard details which have tended to be an elusive concept in most projects can be much more effective with CAD, because of the system's ability to copy and adapt items for local circumstances. This concept can be extended on until, for the first time, a firm can begin to contemplate the build-up of its design expertise in a tangible form that becomes more and more useful as time goes by. No longer do designs have to be completely reinvented from the start.

Yet another layer is already discernable, for we have seen how a national database for building products has already been established. The aim with this is for graphical information and specification data for manufactured products to be mounted and kept up to date on the computer of any design organisation. The data is then readily available for use on any of its designs. This facility will obviously grow with time. Eventually we may see applications for national standards, codes of good practice, example details and so on, so that these too will be widely available in electronic form.

There are problems too. The construction industry is highly fragmented. CAD techniques are currently also fragmented into incompatible programs and equipment, and this state of affairs will continue for some time to come. Too little is being done to overcome this growing problem. There are already signs within the construction industry of a regrouping of design partners, where a main criterion is whether the CAD computers used by the respective firms can 'talk' to one another.

Throughout, it has been stressed that CAD is merely a tool or aid for designers. It may well turn out to be the most powerful weapon that exists in the armoury. But it remains an aid, and the skill with which it is manipulated will determine the amount of benefit or otherwise which devolves on the designer and project.

The main problems appear to be in the selection of a system which best suits the needs of any one organisation, and then in the preparation for, and integration and ongoing management of the system after it arrives. These subjects have been discussed in some detail in the foregoing pages. These are the problems that will continue to loom large in the future.

Useful Addresses

Applied Research of Cambridge Ltd	Wellington House, East Road, Cambridge CB1 1BH, England (Tel: 0223 314041)
Applied Research of Cambridge Inc	765 Cayuga Street, Lewiston, New York 14092, USA (Tel: (716) 754 4380)
Architectural Data Systems Ltd	5 The Laffords, South End, Bradfield, Berks RG7 6JD, England (Tel: 0734 744828)
Building Design Partnership	Vernon Street, Moor Lane, Preston, Lancs PR1 3PQ, England (Tel: 0772 59383)
CSC Ltd	2 Ash Grove, Horton Road, Bradford, England (Tel: 0274 391076)
CalComp Ltd	Cory House, The Ring, Bracknell, Berks RG12 1ER, England (Tel: 0344 50211)
CalComp Inc	2411 West La Palma Avenue, Anaheim, California, CA 82801, USA (Tel: (714) 821 2011)
Cambridge Interactive Systems Ltd (CIS)	Quayside, Cambridge CB5 8AB, England (Tel: 0223 62247)
Computervision Corporation	Computervision Centre, Hayes, Middlesex, England (Tel: 01 561 2626)
Computervision Corporation	201 Burlington Road, Bedford, MA 01730, USA (Tel: (617) 275 1800)
GMW Computers Ltd	Castle Mill, Lower Kings Road, Berkhamsted, Herts HP4 2AD, England (Tel: 044 27 5481)

GMW Computers Inc	1417 4th Avenue, Seattle, Washington 98101, USA (Tel: (206) 467 0660)
Inspectorate EaE Ltd	Computer Systems Div., Currie House, Herbert Walker Avenue, West Docks, Southampton SO1 0HJ, England (Tel: 0703 35611)
Intergraph (Great Britain) Ltd	Albion House, Oxford Street, Newbury, Berks RG13 1JG, England (Tel: 0635 49044)
Intergraph Corporation	One Madison Industrial Park, Huntsville, Alabama 35807, USA (Tel: (205) 772 2000)
Moss Consortium	County Hall, Tower Street, Chichester, W. Sussex, England (Tel: 0243 777573)
Mountford & Laxon Co Ltd	Sharrow House, 20 Anchorage Road, Sutton Coldfield, W. Midlands B74 2PL, England (Tel: 021 354 5389)
Oasys Ltd	13 Fitzroy Street, London W1, England (Tel: 01 636 1531)
Pafec Ltd	Strelley Hall, Strelley, Nottingham NG8 6PE, England (Tel: 0602 292291)
Prime Computers (UK) Ltd	The Hounslow Centre, Lampton Road, Hounslow, Middlesex TW13 1JB, England (Tel: 01 572 7400)

Index